ADVANTAGE SERIES

MICROSOFT®

OUTLOOK® 2000

BRIEF EDITION

Sarah E. Hutchinson

Glen J. Coulthard

InformationTechnology

McGraw-Hill
Irwin

Boston Burr Ridge, IL Dubuque, IA Madison, WI New York San Francisco St. Louis
Bangkok Bogotá Caracas Lisbon London Madrid
Mexico City Milan New Delhi Seoul Singapore Sydney Taipei Toronto

ADVANTAGE
SERIES

MICROSOFT®

OUTLOOK® 2000

BRIEF EDITION

McGraw-Hill Higher Education
*A Division of The **McGraw-Hill** Companies*

MICROSOFT® OUTLOOK® 2000
BRIEF EDITION

This book is printed on acid-free paper.

1 2 3 4 5 6 7 8 9 0 WEB/WEB 9 0 9 8 2 1 0 9

ISBN 0-07-235873-4

Vice president/Editor in chief: *Michael W. Junior*

Publisher: *David Kendric Brake*

Senior sponsoring editor: *Jodi McPherson*

Developmental editor: *Erin Riley*

Associate editor: *Steve Schuetz*

Senior marketing manager: *Jeff Parr*

Project manager: *Christina Thornton-Villagomez*

Production supervisor: *Debra Sylvester*

Freelance design coordinator: *Laurie J. Entringer*

Interior Designer: *AM Design*

Cover Image: © *Schlowsky/Workbook Co/Op Stock*

Senior supplement coordinator: *Marc Mattson*

Compositor: *GTS Graphics*

Typeface: *11/13 Stone Serif*

Printer: *Webcrafters, Inc.*

Library of Congress Cataloging-in-Publication Data

Hutchinson, Sarah E.
Microsoft Outlook 2000 / Sarah E. Hutchinson, Glen J. Coulthard.—Brief ed.
p. cm.—(Advantage series)
Includes index.
ISBN 0-07-235873-4 (softcover : alk. paper)
1. Microsoft Outlook 2. Time management—Computer programs. 3. Personal information management—Computer programs. I. Coulthard, Glen J. II. Title. III. Series.

HD69.T54 H88 2001
005.75'65—dc21 00-038295

INTERNATIONAL EDITION ISBN 0-07-118046-x

http://www.mhhe.com

InformationTechnology

At McGraw-Hill Higher Education, we publish instructional materials targeted at the higher-education market. In an effort to expand the tools of higher learning, we publish texts, lab manuals, study guides, testing materials, software, and multimedia products.

At Irwin/McGraw-Hill (a division of McGraw-Hill Higher Education), we realize that technology will continue to create new media for professors and students to manage resources and communicate information with one another. We strive to provide the most flexible and complete teaching and learning tools available and offer solutions to the changing world of teaching and learning.

Irwin/McGraw-Hill is dedicated to providing the tools for today's instructors and students to successfully navigate the world of Information Technology.

- **Seminar Series**—Irwin/McGraw-Hill's Technology Connection seminar series, offered across the country every year, demonstrate the latest technology products and encourage collaboration among teaching professionals.
- **Osborne/McGraw-Hill**—This division of The McGraw-Hill Companies that is known for its best-selling Internet titles *Harley Hahn's Internet & Web Yellow Pages* and the *Internet Complete Reference*, offers an additional resource for certification and has strategic publishing relationships with corporations such as Corel Corporation and America Online. For more information, visit Osborne at www.osborne.com.
- **Digital Solutions**—Irwin/McGraw-Hill is committed to publishing Digital Solutions. Taking your course online doesn't have to be a solitary venture, nor does it have to be a difficult one. We offer several solutions, which will let you enjoy all the benefits of having course material online. For more information, visit www.mhhe.com/solutions/index.mhtml.
- **Packaging Options**—For more information about our discount options, contact your local Irwin/McGraw-Hill Sales representative at 1-800-338-3987 or visit our Web site at www.mhhe.com/it.

McGraw-Hill
Irwin

Preface
The Advantage Series

Goals/Philosophy

The Advantage Series presents the **What, Why,** and **How** of computer application skills to today's students. Each lab manual is built upon an efficient learning model that provides students and faculty with complete coverage of the most powerful software packages available today.

Approach

The Advantage Series builds upon an efficient learning model that provides students and faculty with complete coverage and enhances critical thinking skills. This case-based, "problem-solving" approach teaches the What, Why, and How of computer application skills.

The Advantage Series introduces the **"Feature-Method-Practice"** layered approach. The **Feature** describes the command and tells the importance of that command. The **Method** shows students how to perform the Feature. The **Practice** allows students to apply the feature in a keystroke exercise.

About the Series

The Advantage Series offers *three levels* of instruction. Each level builds upon the previous level. The following are the three levels of instructions:

Brief: Covers the basics of the application, contains two to four chapters, and is typically 120–190 pages long.

Introductory: Includes the material in the Brief lab manual plus two to three additional chapters. The Introductory lab manuals are approximately 300 pages long and prepare students for the *Microsoft Office User Specialist Proficient Exam (MOUS Certification).*

Complete: Includes the Introductory lab manual plus an additional five chapters of advanced level content. The Complete lab manuals are approximately 600 pages in length and prepare students to take the *Microsoft Office User Specialist Expert Exam (MOUS Certification).*

Approved Microsoft Courseware

APPROVED COURSEWARE

Use of the Microsoft Office User Specialist Approved Courseware Logo on this product signifies that it has been independently reviewed and approved as complying with the following standards: Acceptable coverage of all content related to the Microsoft Office Exam entitled *Microsoft Outlook 2000* and sufficient performance-based exercises that relate closely to all required content, based on sampling of text. For further information on Microsoft's MOUS certification program please visit Microsoft's Web site at http://www.microsoft.com/office/traincert/.

About the Book

Each lab manual features the following:

- ***Learning Objectives:*** At the beginning of each chapter, a list of action-oriented objectives is presented detailing what is expected of the students.
- ***Chapters:*** Each lab manual is divided into chapters.
- ***Modules:*** Each chapter contains three to five independent modules, requiring approximately 30–45 minutes each to complete. Although we recommend you complete an entire chapter before proceeding, you may skip or rearrange the order of these modules to best suit your learning needs.

Case Study

- ***Case Studies:*** Each chapter begins with a Case Study. The student is introduced to a fictitious person or company and their immediate problem or opportunity. Throughout the chapter, students obtain the knowledge and skills necessary to meet the challenges presented in the Case Study. At the end of each chapter, students are asked to solve problems directly related to the Case Study.
- ***Feature-Method-Practice:*** Each chapter highlights our unique "Feature-Method-Practice" layered approach. The ***Feature*** layer describes the command or technique and explains its importance and relevance. The ***Method*** layer shows you how to perform the procedure, while the ***Practice*** layer lets you apply the feature in a hands-on, step-by-step exercise.

1 2 3

- ***Instructions:*** The numbered step-by-step progression for all hands-on examples and exercises is clearly identified. Students will find it surprisingly easy to follow the logical sequence of keystrokes and mouse clicks and no longer worry about missing a step.

In Addition

- ***In Addition Boxes:*** These content boxes are placed strategically throughout the chapter and provide information on advanced topics that are beyond the scope of the current discussion.
- ***Self-Check Boxes:*** At the end of each module, a brief self-check question appears for students to test their comprehension of the material. Answers to these questions appear in the Appendix.
- ***Chapter Review:*** The *Command Summary* and *Key Terms* provide an excellent review of the chapter content and prepare students for the short-answer, true-false, and multiple-choice questions at the end of each chapter.

Easy
Moderate
Difficult

- ***Hands-On Projects:*** Each chapter concludes with six hands-on projects rated according to their difficulty level. The *easy* and *moderate* projects use a running-case approach, whereby the same person or company appears at the end of each chapter in a particular tutorial. The two *difficult* or *on your own* projects provide greater latitude in applying the software to a variety of creative problem-solving situations.
- ***Appendix: Microsoft Windows Quick Reference:*** Each lab manual contains a Microsoft Windows Quick Reference. This Quick reference teaches students the fundamentals of using a mouse and a keyboard, illustrates how to interact with a dialog box, and describes the fundamentals of how to use the Office 2000 Help System.

Features of This Lab Manual

Instructions: The numbered step-by-step progression for all hands-on examples and exercises are clearly identified. Students will find it surprisingly easy to follow the logical sequence of keystrokes and mouse clicks, and no longer worry about missing a step.

8. To return to a multicolumn list format:
   CLICK: down arrow beside the Views button
   CHOOSE: List

9. Let's open one of the documents in the list area:
   DOUBLE-CLICK: WRD140
   The dialog box disappears and the document is loaded into the application window. (*Note:* The "WRD140" filename reflects that this document is used in module 1.4 of the Word learning guide.)

10. Close the document before proceeding.

In Addition Boxes: These content boxes are placed strategically throughout the chapter and provide information on topics that are beyond the scope of the current discussion.

In Addition
Storing and Retrieving Files on Web Servers

With the appropriate network connection, you can open and save Word documents on the Internet. In the Open or Save As dialog boxes, click the Web Folders button ( ) in the Places bar or select an FTP Internet site from the *Look in* drop-down list. This feature allows you to share and update Word documents with users from around the world.

Self-Check Boxes: At the end of each module, a brief self-check question appears for students to test their comprehension of the material. Answers to these questions appear in the Appendix.

1.4 Self Check In the Open and Save As dialog boxes, how do the List and Details views differ?

1.5 Previewing and Printing

This module focuses on outputting your document creations. Most commonly, you will print a document for inclusion into a report or other such document.

1.5.1 Previewing a Document

Feature-Method-Practice: Each chapter highlights our unique "**Feature-Method-Practice**" layered approach. The ***Feature*** layer describes the command or technique and persuades you of its importance and relevance. The ***Method*** layer shows you how to perform the procedure, while the ***Practice*** layer lets you apply the feature in a hands-on, step-by-step exercise.

FEATURE
Before sending a document to the printer, you can preview it using a full-page display that closely resembles the printed version. In this Preview display mode, you can move through the document pages, and zoom in and out on desired areas.

METHOD
CLICK: Print Preview button ( ), or
CHOOSE: File, Print Preview

PRACTICE
You will now open a relatively large document and then preview it on the screen.

Case Studies: Each chapter begins with a Case Study. Throughout the chapter, students obtain the knowledge and skills necessary to meet the challenges presented in the Case Study. At the end of each chapter, students are asked to solve problems directly related to the Case Study.

Chapters: Each lab manual is divided into chapters. Each chapter is composed of 2–5 ***Modules.*** Each module is composed of one or more ***Lessons.***

New Design: The ***new*** Advantage Series design offers a shaded area where the Feature-Method-Practice and numbered step-by-step instructions maintain the learning focus.

Case Study

1-on-1 Tutoring Services

Dean Shearwater is helping to pay his university tuition by tutoring other university and high school students. Over the last two years, he has developed an excellent reputation for making complex topics simple and easy to remember. While he is an excellent tutor, last year he didn't earn as much as he had expected.

Dean thinks his lackluster earnings can be attributed to poor advertising and inadequate record keeping. This year, he has decided to operate his tutoring services more like a real business. His first priority is to learn how to use Microsoft Word so that he can prepare advertising materials, send faxes and memos, and organize his student notes.

In this chapter, you and Dean learn how to create simple documents from scratch, use built-in document templates, edit documents, and use the Undo command. You also learn how to preview and print your work.

1.1 Getting Started with Word

Microsoft Word 2000 is a **word processing** program that enables you to create, edit, format, and print many types of documents including résumés and cover letters, reports and proposals, World Wide Web pages, and more. By the time you complete this learning guide, you will be skilled in creating all types of documents and in getting them to look the way you want. In this module, you load Microsoft Word and proceed through a guided tour of its primary components.

1.1.1 Loading and Exiting Word

FEATURE

You load Word from the Windows Start menu, accessed by clicking the Start button (Start) on the taskbar. Because Word requires a significant amount of memory, you should always exit the application when you are finished doing your work. Most Windows applications allow you to close their windows by clicking the Close button (×) appearing in the top right-hand corner.

Teaching Resources

The following is a list of supplemental material that can be used to teach this course.

Skills Assessment

Irwin/McGraw-Hill offers two innovative systems that can be used with the Advantage Series, ATLAS and **SimNet,** which take skills assessment testing beyond the basics with pre- and post-assessment capability.

- **ATLAS—(Active Testing and Learning Assessment Software)**—ATLAS is our tool for **live** application skills assessment. ATLAS allows students to perform tasks while working live within the office applications environment. ATLAS is Web-enabled and customizable to meet the needs of your course. ATLAS is available for Office 2000.
- **SimNet—(Simulated Network Assessment Product)**—SimNet permits you to test the actual software skills students learn about the Microsoft Office Applications in a **simulated** environment. SimNet is Web-enabled and is available for Office 97 and Office 2000.

Instructor's Resource Kits

The Instructor's Resource Kit provides professors with all of the ancillary material needed to teach a course. Irwin/McGraw-Hill is committed to providing instructors with the most effective instructional resources available. Many of these resources are available at our **Information Technology Supersite** at www.mhhe.com/it. Our Instructor's Resource Kits are available on CD-ROM and contain the following:

- **Diploma by Brownstone**—This computerized testing system is the most flexible, powerful, and easy-to-use system available in higher education. The diploma system allows professors to create an exam as a printed version, as a LAN-based Online version, and as an Internet version. Diploma includes grade-book features, which automate the entire testing process.
- **Instructor's Manual**—This resource includes:
  —Solutions to all lessons and end-of-chapter material
  —Teaching Tips
  —Teaching Strategies
  —Additional Exercises
- **Student Data Files**—To use the Advantage Series, students must have data files to complete practice and test lessons. The instructor and students using this text in classes are granted the right to post the student files on any network or stand-alone computer, or to distribute the files on individual diskettes. The student files may be downloaded from our IT Supersite at www.mhhe.com/it.
- **Series Web Site**—Available at www.mhhe.com/cit/apps/adv/.

Digital Solutions

PageOut Lite—Allows instructors to create their own basic Web sites hosted by McGraw-Hill. PageOut Lite includes three basic templates that automatically convert typed material into HTML Web Pages. Using PageOut Lite an instructor can set up a Home page, Web links, and a basic course syllabus and lecture notes.

PageOut—Irwin/McGraw-Hill's Course Webster Development Center. PageOut allows an instructor to create a more complex course Webster with an interactive syllabus and some course management features. Like PageOut Lite, PageOut converts typed material to HTML. For more information, please visit the PageOut Web site at www.mhla.net/pageout.

OLC/Series Web Sites—Online Learning Centers (OLCs)/Series Sites are accessible through our Supersite at www.mhhe.com/it. Our OLC/Series Sites provide pedagogical features and supplements for our titles online. Students can point and click their way to key terms, learning objectives, chapter overviews, PowerPoint slides, exercises, and Web links.

The McGraw-Hill Learning Architecture (MHLA)—A complete course delivery system. MHLA gives professors ownership in the way digital content is presented to the class through online quizzing, student collaboration, course administration, and content management. For a walkthrough of MHLA, visit the MHLA Web site at www.mhla.net.

Packaging Options

For more information about our discount options, contact your local Irwin/McGraw-Hill Sales representative at 1-800-338-3987 or visit our Web site at www.mhhe.com/it.

Acknowledgments

This series of tutorials is the direct result of the teamwork and heart of many people. We sincerely thank the reviewers, instructors, and students who have shared their comments and suggestions with us over the past few years. We do read them! With their valuable feedback, our tutorials have evolved into the product you see before you.

Many thanks go to Trisha O'Shea and Carrie Berkshire from Irwin/McGraw-Hill whose management helped to get this book produced in a timely and efficient manner. Special recognition goes to all of the individuals mentioned in the credits at the beginning of this tutorial. And finally, to the many others who weren't directly involved in this project but who have stood by us the whole way, we appreciate your encouragement and support.

The Advantage Team

Special thanks go out to our contributing members on the Advantage team.

Verlaine Murphy
Walt Musekamp
Ingrid Neumann
Catherine Schuler

Write to Us

We welcome your response to this tutorial, for we are trying to make it as useful a learning tool as possible. Please contact us at

Sarah E. Hutchinson—sarah-hutchinson@home.com

Glen J. Coulthard—glen@coulthard.com

Contents

GETTING STARTED WITH OUTLOOK — CHAPTER 1

MANAGING EVERYDAY INFORMATION — CHAPTER 2

CHAPTER 3 WORKING WITH E-MAIL

ADVANTAGE SERIES

MICROSOFT®

OUTLOOK® 2000

BRIEF EDITION

Microsoft Outlook 2000

Getting Started with Outlook

Chapter One

Chapter Outline

Learning Objectives

After reading this chapter, you will be able to:

- Describe the features and capabilities of Microsoft Outlook
- Navigate Outlook's components and display data in different formats
- Use the Contacts tool to add, view, and print contact items
- Use the Notes tool to create electronic sticky notes
- Obtain helpful information using the Office Assistant and Outlook's Help window

Case Study

SilverHome Accommodation

SilverHome Accommodation is located in a quaint ski village on Silver Star Mountain in Vernon, British Columbia. With over 100 homes, suites, and chalets from which to choose, owners Narissa and Stan Byron take pride in offering the finest accommodations to suit the needs of their guests. To date, Narissa and Stan have been keeping track of their numerous business contacts in a paper notebook. Frustrated with their constantly changing contact list and the numerous sticky notes pasted around their office, they have decided to learn more about these features in Microsoft Outlook 2000.

In this chapter, you and the Byrons begin by loading and touring Outlook's components. You will then use the Contacts tool to add, edit, view, and print contact information. Finally, you will create, manage, and customize note items, and practice navigating Outlook's Help system.

1.1 Touring Outlook

Having access to accurate information about the people you deal with and maintaining those relationships is vital. **Microsoft Outlook 2000** is a personal information and e-mail manager for tracking such everyday information as appointments, contact information, tasks, notes, and of course, e-mail. It includes seven tools for keeping your life in order:

Outlook Today provides a snapshot of activities that relate to the current day, including a list of appointments, a list of tasks that you would like to perform, and an indication of whether you've received e-mail.

Inbox is an electronic mail program that lets you compose, send and receive, and manage e-mail messages.

Calendar is an electronic appointment calendar that helps you keep track of important dates such as meetings, project schedules, vacations, and birthdays.

Contacts is an electronic address book in which you can store personal and business contact information, such as name, address, phone and fax numbers, and e-mail addresses.

Tasks helps you keep track of tasks that need to be performed, including their priority, who will perform them, and when they should be completed.

Journal records when events take place on a single timeline. You can customize Journal to keep track of such events as phone calls, e-mail messages, faxes, file updates, and meetings.

Notes is an online version of sticky notes that you can post anywhere within Outlook or on the Windows desktop.

1.1.1 Loading and Exiting Outlook

FEATURE

You can load Outlook 2000 from the desktop, from the Start menu, or from the Quick Launch toolbar, which is located on the Windows taskbar.

METHOD

To load Outlook:

- CLICK: Start button (Start)
  CHOOSE: Programs, Microsoft Outlook, or
- CLICK: Launch Microsoft Outlook icon () on the Quick Launch toolbar, or
- DOUBLE-CLICK: Microsoft Outlook icon () on the Windows desktop

To exit Outlook:

- CHOOSE: File, Exit

PRACTICE

In this lesson, you load Microsoft Outlook from the Start menu. You also practice switching among Outlook folders and changing the size of icons on the Outlook Bar.

Setup: Ensure that Microsoft Outlook is installed on your computer.

1. To load Outlook from the Start menu:
   CLICK: Start button Start
   CHOOSE: Programs, Microsoft Outlook

2 If the Office Assistant and the tip window appear, as shown to the right, do the following:
CHOOSE: Help, Hide the Office Assistant from the Menu bar
(*Note:* In the future, when you need help accomplishing a particular task, you call up the Assistant by clicking the Microsoft Outlook Help button (?) on the Standard toolbar.)

3 Maximize the Outlook application window. Your screen should now appear similar to Figure 1.1, although the Information Viewer area will differ. The application window is composed of the Title bar, Menu bar, Standard toolbar, Outlook Bar, and Information Viewer.

Figure 1.1
Loading Microsoft Outlook

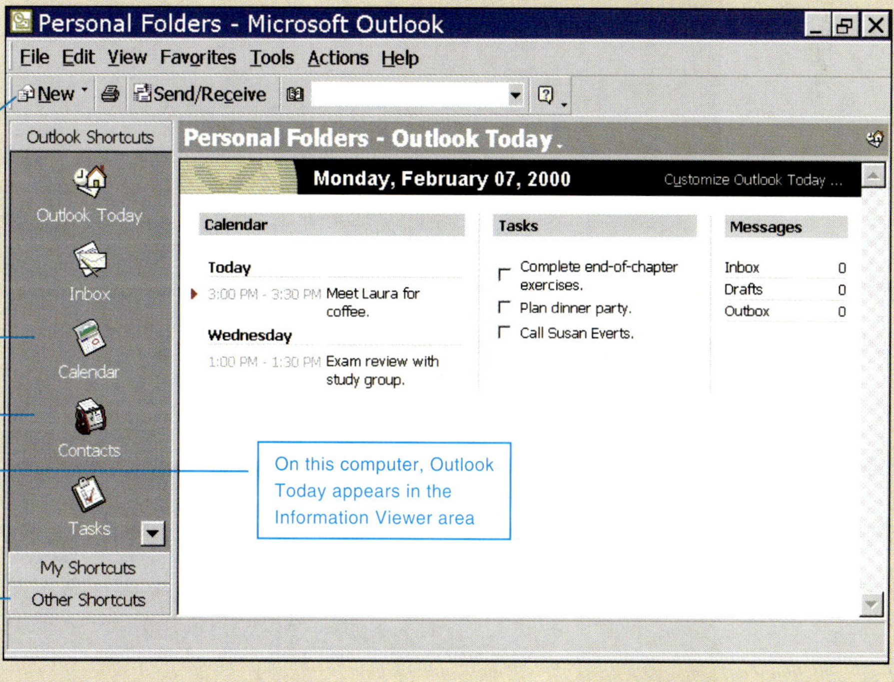

4 Continue to the next lesson.

1.1.2 Navigating Outlook's Components

FEATURE
The Outlook Bar provides single-click access to Outlook's tools and other resources on your computer. Initially, the Outlook Bar contains three groups—Outlook Shortcuts, My Shortcuts, and Other Shortcuts—containing the icons Microsoft thinks you'll use the most often. You can customize the Outlook Bar by adding and removing icons and by changing their size.

METHOD

- To navigate among Outlook's components:
  CLICK: group button to display its contents
  CLICK: desired shortcut icon
- To change the size of the icons in the Outlook Bar:
  RIGHT-CLICK: the background of the Outlook Bar
  CHOOSE: Large Icons or Small Icons

PRACTICE
In this lesson, you practice navigating among the different Outlook tools and changing the size of the icons in the Outlook Bar.

Setup: Ensure that you've completed the previous lesson and that Microsoft Outlook is loaded.

1. To ensure that your screen appears similar to Figure 1.1:
   CLICK: Outlook Shortcuts group button
   CLICK: Outlook Today icon ( ) in the Outlook Bar

2. Now let's access the Contacts tool.
   CLICK: Contacts icon ( ) in the Outlook Bar
   Outlook refers to the information it manages, such as an address, appointment, or e-mail message, as *items*. As pictured in Figure 1.2, several contact items are currently displaying in the Information Viewer area. Note that the Standard toolbar has changed. Each Outlook tool has its own Standard toolbar and unique menu commands.

Figure 1.2
Contacts folder:
Phone List layout

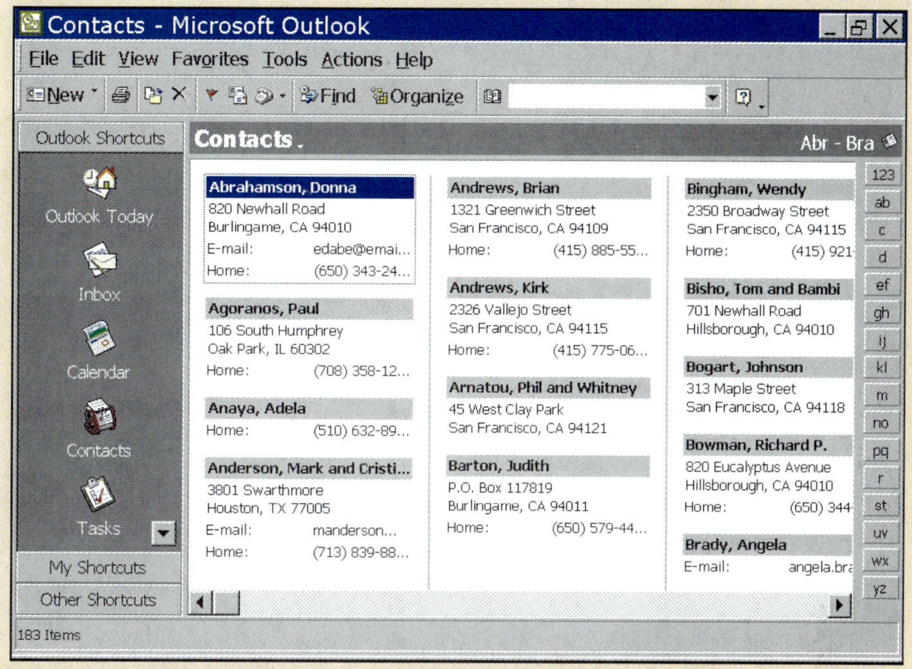

3. On your own, click the other icons in the Outlook Bar to see how the Information Viewer area changes. As you do so, note that the Standard toolbar adapts to the current tool.

4. Let's view the icons in the My Shortcuts group.
CLICK: My Shortcuts group button in the Outlook Bar
By default, the My Shortcuts group provides access to e-mail messages that you're still working on, are waiting to deliver, or have already sent. Also, any new folders that you create are initially stored in the My Shortcuts group.[1]

5. On your own, display the icons contained in the Other Shortcuts group. You can use the icons in this group—My Computer, My Documents, and Favorites—to access resources outside Outlook such as the documents you work with.

6. Before continuing
CLICK: Outlook Shortcuts group button in the Outlook Bar
CLICK: Outlook Today icon () in the Outlook Bar

7. Let's practice changing the size of icons in the Outlook Bar.
RIGHT-CLICK: in the background of the Outlook Bar
CHOOSE: Small Icons from the right-click menu
All the shortcuts in the Outlook Shortcuts group are now visible.

---

[1]We describe creating folders in Chapter 2.

8. To display large icons:
RIGHT-CLICK: in the background of the Outlook Bar
CHOOSE: Large Icons
(*Note:* While displaying large icons, you can scroll through a long list of icons using the up arrow (▲) and down arrow (▼) buttons that appear in the Outlook Bar.)

9. Continue to the next lesson.

1.1.3 Switching Views

FEATURE
As you already know, after you click an icon in the Outlook Bar, its corresponding information appears in the Information Viewer. You can customize how information is presented in the Information Viewer by selecting an alternate view of the data. Each of Outlook's tools comes with anywhere from 5 to 12 views.

METHOD
CHOOSE: View, Current View, *option*

PRACTICE
In this lesson, you practice switching views.

Setup: Ensure that you've completed the previous lesson and that the contents of the Outlook Today folder are displaying.

1. Let's practice switching views using the Contacts tool. To begin:
CLICK: Contacts icon in the Outlook bar

2. In Figure 1.2, shown earlier, the items in the Contacts folder are displaying using the Address Cards view. On your computer, if the Contacts folder is using a different view:
CHOOSE: View, Current View, Address Cards

3. To switch to the Phone List view:
CHOOSE: View, Current View, Phone List
Figure 1.3 provides an example of the Phone List layout.

Figure 1.3
Contacts folder:
Phone List view

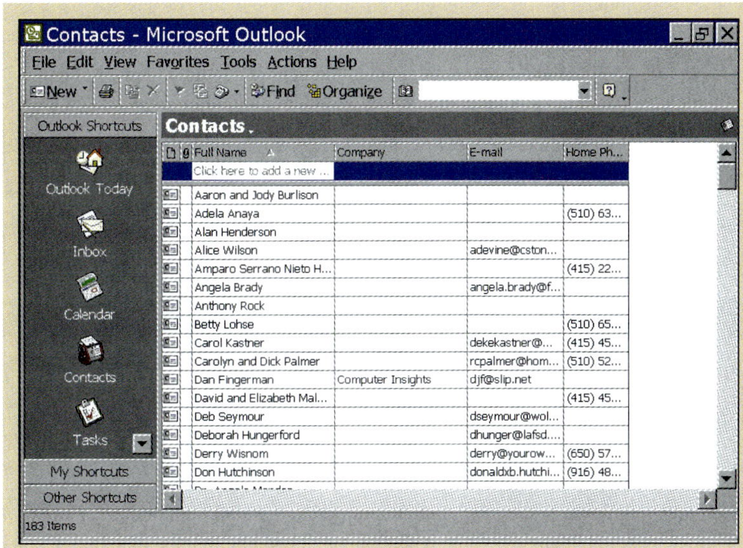

4. On your own, practice switching views using the Calendar, Tasks, Journal, and Notes tools.

5. To prepare for the next lesson:
CLICK: Outlook Today icon ( ) in the Outlook Bar

1.1.4 Previewing Your Day

FEATURE
The Outlook Today tool (shown earlier in Figure 1.1) provides a nice overview of today's activities by displaying upcoming appointments, your current "to do" list, and the status of your e-mail messages. Outlook Today obtains its information by scanning the Calendar, Tasks, and Inbox folders and displaying items related to the current week. To customize the look of the Outlook Today folder, you must click the Customize Outlook Today hyperlink.

METHOD
To customize the appearance of the Outlook Today folder:

1. CLICK: Customize Outlook Today hyperlink
2. CLICK: Save Changes hyperlink to save your changes and return to the Outlook Today folder

PRACTICE

In this lesson, you change the appearance of the Outlook Today folder.

Setup: Ensure that you've completed the previous lessons in this module and that the contents of the Outlook Today folder are displaying.

1 To customize the Outlook Today folder:
CLICK: Customize Outlook Today hyperlink
Your screen should now appear similar to Figure 1.4. Using this screen, you can specify whether to display the Outlook Today folder when you load Outlook, and also what folders, calendar days, and tasks you want Outlook Today to show. You can also change the look of the Outlook Today folder by selecting an alternate style.

Figure 1.4
Customizing Outlook Today

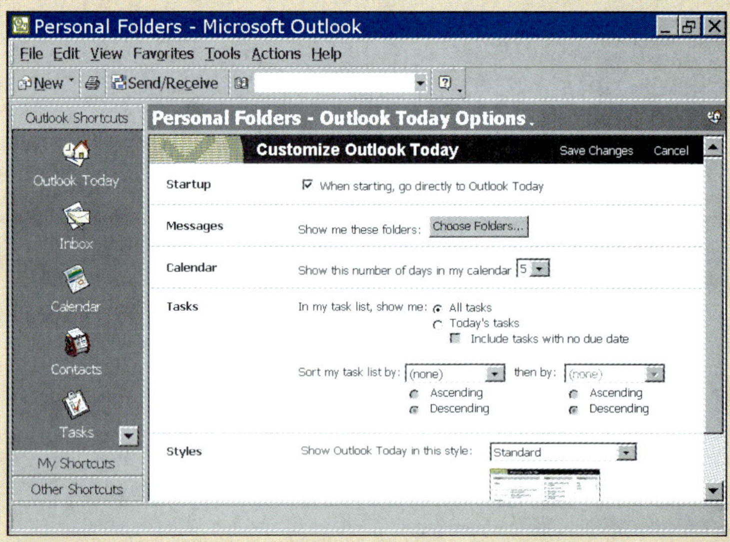

2 Let's change the look of the Outlook Today folder. When Outlook is first installed, the Standard style is applied to the Outlook Today folder. Let's apply the Winter style.
CLICK: drop-down arrow in the *Styles* area
CHOOSE: Winter from the drop-down list
Note that you can preview the style in the graphic located in the *Styles* area.

3 To save your changes and redisplay the Outlook Today folder:
CLICK: Save Changes hyperlink (located at the top of the Information Viewer)
Figure 1.5 provides an example of the Outlook Today folder after applying the Winter style.

Figure 1.5
Applying the Winter style to the Outlook Today folder

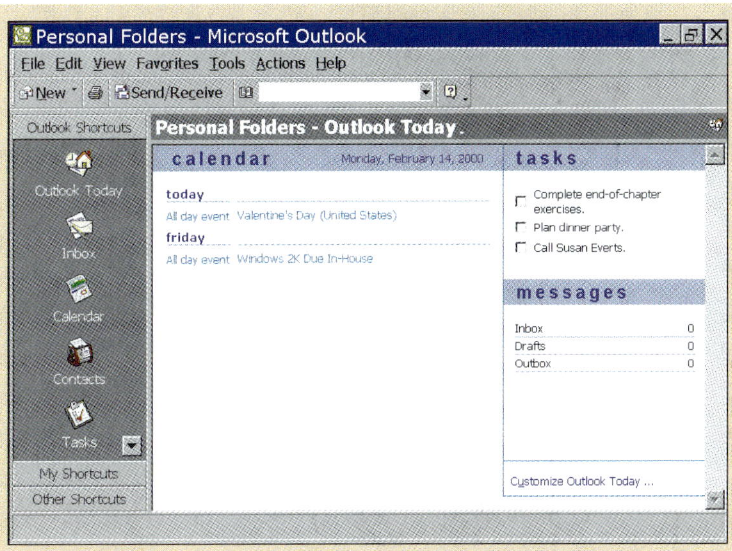

4 On your own, apply the style of your choice to the Outlook Today folder.

1.1 Self Check Why is it important to know how to change the current view in Outlook?

1.2 Managing Contact Information

Even if you work alone, you probably still deal with lots of people including people you buy things from or sell things to, doctors, friends, family, and so on. What most people need is an easy-to-use tool for storing basic data such as names, addresses, and contact numbers plus the flexibility to accommodate more detailed information such as birthdays and anniversaries. Using Outlook's Contacts tool, you can store as little or as much information as you want about a particular contact, as well as sort the information and print it in a variety of formats. In this module, you practice entering and managing contact items using the Contacts tool.

1.2.1 Adding and Editing Contact Items

FEATURE
When you initiate the command to add a contact, Outlook displays five tabs for collecting information, two of which you will use the most. Use the *General* tab to fill in basic information such as name, address, phone, and e-mail data, and the *Details* tab to fill in more personal information such as department, profession, nickname, birthday, and anniversary. Once you've saved a contact item to your contact list, you can easily edit it or delete it when it's no longer needed.

METHOD
To add a contact item:

1. CLICK: Contacts icon ( ) in the Outlook Bar
2. CLICK: New Contact button ( ) on the Standard toolbar
3. CLICK: the tab you want to use and then fill in the relevant blanks
4. CLICK: Save and Close button on the Standard toolbar

To edit a contact item:

1. DOUBLE-CLICK: a contact item and then make your changes
2. CLICK: Save and Close button on the Standard toolbar

To delete a contact item:

1. CLICK: a contact item in the Information Viewer to select it
2. CLICK: Delete button ( ) on the Standard toolbar

PRACTICE
In this lesson, you will use the Contacts tool to collect information about a fictitious contact. After editing the information, you will then delete the contact from your contact database.

Setup: Ensure that Outlook is loaded.

1 To access the Contacts tool:
CLICK: Contacts icon ( ) in the Outlook Bar
A list of your stored contacts, if any exist, should now appear in the Information Viewer.

2 To add a new contact:
CLICK: New Contact button ( ) on the Standard toolbar
The Contact window (Figure 1.6) should now appear. (*Note:* If the Contact window isn't maximized, click its Maximize button.)

Figure 1.6

The Contact window: *General* tab

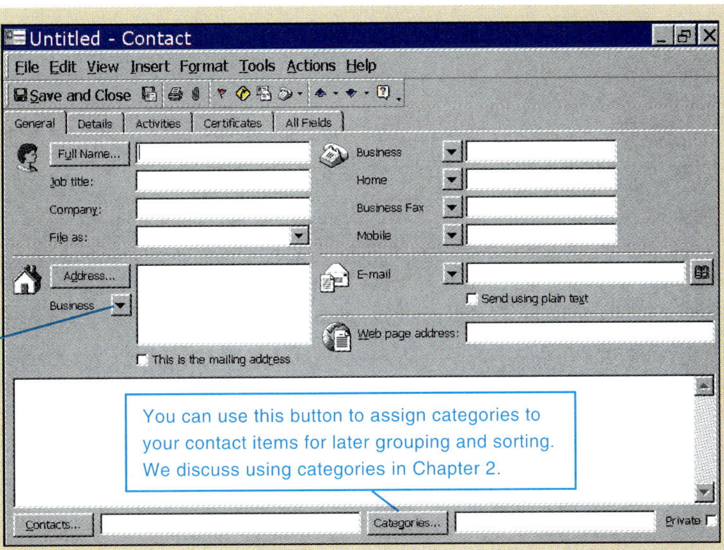

Note that "Business" appears to the left of the drop-down arrow. To enter a home address for a given contact, use the drop-down arrow to select "Home" and then type in the new address.

You can use this button to assign categories to your contact items for later grouping and sorting. We discuss using categories in Chapter 2.

3. The insertion point is blinking in the *Full Name* field. You can either type the contact name in directly or click the Full Name command button to enter the name using a structured form. Let's use the form this time.
CLICK: Full Name command button
The following dialog box should now appear:

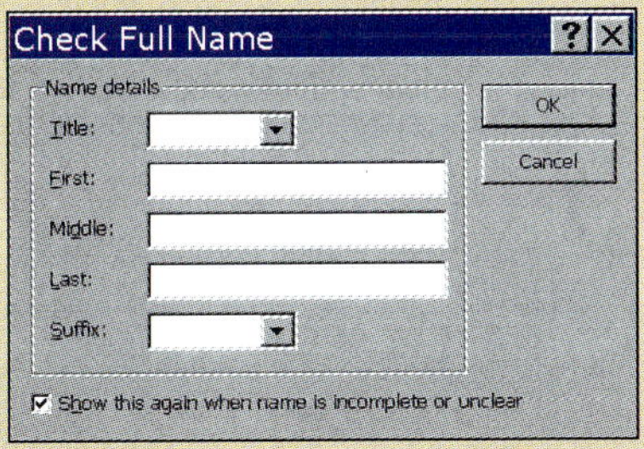

4. To supply title information, you can either type the title in directly or select it from the drop-down list.
CLICK: *Title* drop-down arrow
SELECT: Dr. from the *Title* drop-down list

5. To supply the remaining information:
CLICK: in the *First* text box
TYPE: **William**
CLICK: in the *Last* text box
TYPE: **Longnose**

OUTLOOK

6. To leave the Check Full Name dialog box:
CLICK: OK command button
Note that "Longnose, William" is displaying in the *File as* text box. If you want Dr. Longnose to be filed under an alternate name such as "Doctor" or "Family Practitioner," simply click in the *File as* text box and then type in the alternate name.

7. In this step, you supply Dr. Longnose's address information. Rather than use the Address command button, let's type the address information directly into the *Address* text box. Do the following:
CLICK: in the *Address* text box
TYPE: **120 Elephantine Way**
PRESS: ENTER
TYPE: **Trunkville, NY 60521**
Note that "Business" is displaying beneath the Address command button. If you also wanted to store Dr. Longnose's home address, you would click the drop-down arrow that appears to the right of "Business" and then select Home from the drop-down list.

8. To use Dr. Longnose's business address for mailing in your payments, ensure that *This is the mailing address* check box is selected. This check box is located beneath the *Address* text box.

9. Numerous options are available in the phone area. By default, fields for Business, Home, Business Fax, and Mobile are displayed. To change a field, click the down arrow that appears next to the option and then choose an alternate field name. To see the list of field names that you can choose from:
CLICK: the down arrow that appears to the right of Mobile
Several options appear in the drop-down list.

10. To continue without making a change:
PRESS: ESC

11. To enter Dr. Longnose's business number:
CLICK: in the text box to the right of the *Business* field
TYPE: **925-222-1010**
(*Note:* You can type the number using whatever format you want. Outlook will automatically apply its own formatting to the number.)

12. To enter Dr. Longnose's e-mail address:
CLICK: in the *E-mail* text box
TYPE: **longnose@inthewild.com**

13 The large text box on the bottom of the form is used for typing in whatever you want, such as directions or reminders to yourself.[2]
CLICK: in the large text box on the bottom of the form
TYPE: **Dr. Longnose only accepts cash or checks.**

14 Before saving this contact item, let's take a look at the *Details* tab.
CLICK: *Details* tab
Your screen should now appear similar to Figure 1.7.

Figure 1.7
The Contact window: *Details* tab

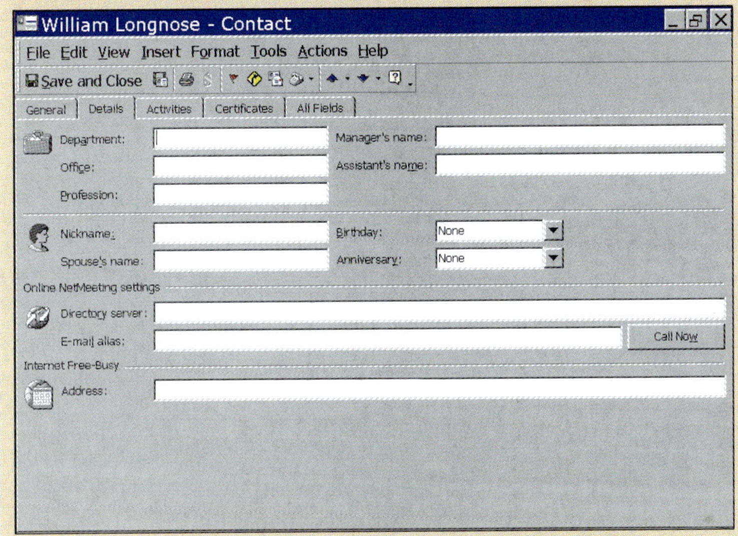

15 Let's take a look at the *Activities* tab.
CLICK: *Activities* tab
Your screen should now appear similar to Figure 1.8. The *Activities* tab is used for listing other Outlook items that relate to your contact, such as all the e-mail messages you've sent to or received from your contact. When you click the *Activities* tab, Outlook will automatically begin a search for all Outlook items that relate to your contact. If you have lots of items stored in Outlook, this search may take a long time. When the search is complete, the results will display in the blank area below. However, since you've just added Dr. Longnose's information, no items will display in the result area.

OUTLOOK

---

[2]You can also format the text using buttons on the Formatting toolbar, which is very similar to the Formatting toolbar found in Word 2000. To display the Formatting toolbar, right-click an existing toolbar and then choose Formatting from the right-click menu.

Figure 1.8
The Contact window: *Activities* tab

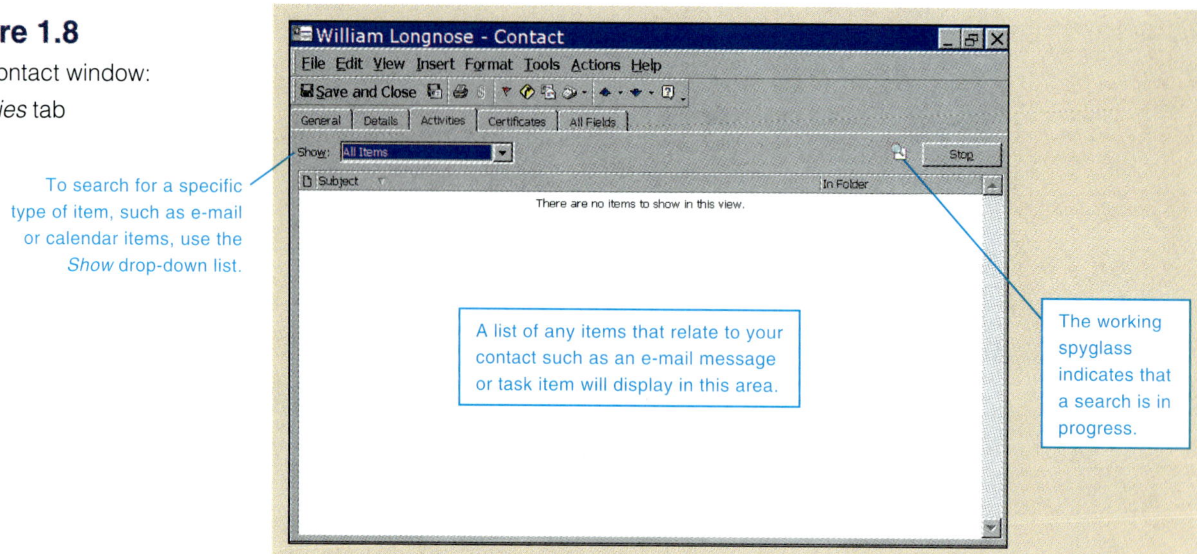

16 Let's save Dr. Longnose's contact information.
CLICK: Save and Close button on the Standard toolbar
You should now see Dr. Longnose's contact information in the Information Viewer. If not, drag the scroll bars in the Information Viewer until his contact information appears.

17 Because contact information changes frequently, it's important to know how to edit existing contacts. Let's edit Dr. Longnose's information and then make a change to the address field.
DOUBLE-CLICK: Dr. Longnose's information in the Information Viewer
SELECT: "120" in the *Address* text box
TYPE: **130**
CLICK: Save and Close button on the Standard toolbar

18 So that your contact list isn't cluttered with fictitious information, let's delete Dr. Longnose's information from your contact database:
CLICK: Dr. Longnose's information in the Information Viewer, if it isn't selected already
CLICK: Delete button (☒) on the Standard toolbar

19 Continue to the next lesson.

In Addition
Manually Recording an Activity in Journal

As you learned in this lesson, when editing a contact item, you can use the ***Activities*** tab to display a list of Outlook items related to the contact. There may be times when you'll want to manually record an activity that you have with a contact, such as a phone call, so that it will appear in the Activities list. To do so, open the contact item or select it in the Information Viewer and then choose Actions, New Journal Entry for Contact. Then, select the type of activity from the ***Entry type*** drop-down list and make selections from the ***Start*** and ***Duration*** drop-down lists. Then, type in a description of the activity in the large text box below.

1.2.2 Viewing and Sorting a Contact List

FEATURE

By default, your contact list displays using the Address Cards view and is sorted in order by the File As field. You can easily change these display settings to suit your needs.

METHOD

- To select an alternate view for your contact list:
  CHOOSE: View, Current View, *option*
- To sort your contact list into an alternate order:
  CHOOSE: View, Current View, Customize Current View
  CLICK: Sort command button
  SELECT: a field from the *Sort items by* drop-down list
  SELECT: *Ascending* or *Descending* option button
  CLICK: OK command button to leave the Sort dialog box
  CLICK: OK command button to leave the View Summary dialog box

PRACTICE

You will now add three fictitious contacts to your contacts folder and then practice switching views and sort orders.

Setup: Ensure that Outlook is loaded and that your contact list is displaying in the Information Viewer.

1. On your own, add the following business contacts to your contact database:

   Mr. Ronald Yawn
   504 Sleepy Lane
   Restland, IL 95207
   Business phone: **(817) 321-3211**
   E-mail address: **ryawn@bignet.com**
   File as: **Practice 1**

   Ms. Yolanda Yoller
   22195 Yollister Place
   Yollicker, NY 20111
   E-mail address: **yyoller@bignet.com**
   File as: **Practice 2**

   Miss Susie Seuss
   14 Green Eggs Drive
   Hamville, TN 12311
   Business phone: **(510) 594-1127**
   E-mail address: **susieseuss@bignet.com**
   File as: **Practice 3**

2. Let's display your contact list using the Phone List view.
   CHOOSE: View, Current View, Phone List
   Your contact list should be displaying across columns and rows.

3. CHOOSE: View, Current View, Address Cards
   Below we show how your three practice records look in the Address Cards view.

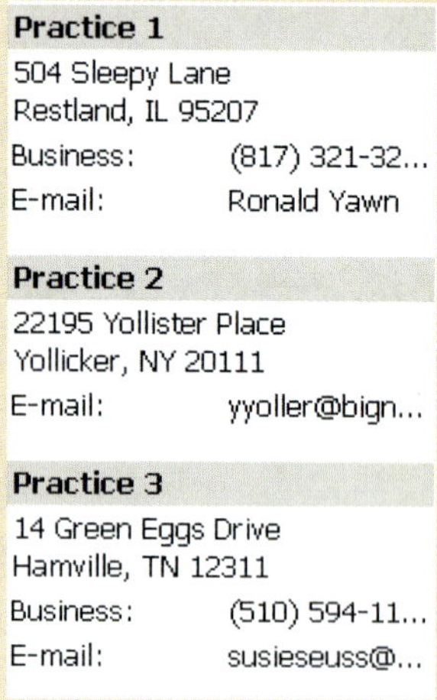

4 Note that your contact list is displaying in order by the File As field. Let's display your contact list in order by the E-mail field.
CHOOSE: View, Current View, Customize Current View
The View Summary dialog box should now appear. Note that "File As" appears next to the Sort command button.

5 CLICK: Sort command button
The Sort dialog box should now appear, as shown in Figure 1.9.

Figure 1.9
Sort dialog box

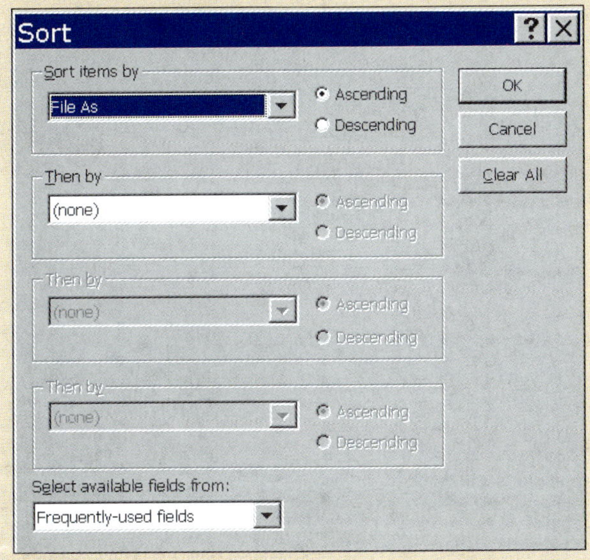

6 To sort your contact list into order by the E-mail field:
SELECT: E-mail from the *Sort items by* drop-down list
CLICK: OK command button
Note that "E-mail" now appears next to the Sort command button.

7 To display your contact list:
CLICK: OK command button
Your contact list is now sorted into order by the E-mail field.

8 On your own, sort your contact list back into order by the File As field.

1.2.3 Printing a Contact List

FEATURE

For those times when you're away from your computer, but still need access to your contact list, consider printing a copy. No matter what tool you're using in Outlook, the same basic steps apply to print your work.

METHOD

1. CHOOSE: File, Print, or
   CLICK: Print button ( ) on the Standard toolbar
2. SELECT: a style in the *Print Style* area
3. SELECT: what to print in the *Print range* area
4. CLICK: OK command button

PRACTICE

In this lesson, you print your contact list.

Setup: Ensure that you've completed the previous lessons in this module and that your contact list is displaying in Address Cards view. Also, your contact list should be displaying in order by the File As field.

1 CHOOSE: File, Print
The Print dialog box should now appear on your screen (Figure 1.10). Note the options available in the *Print Style* list box.

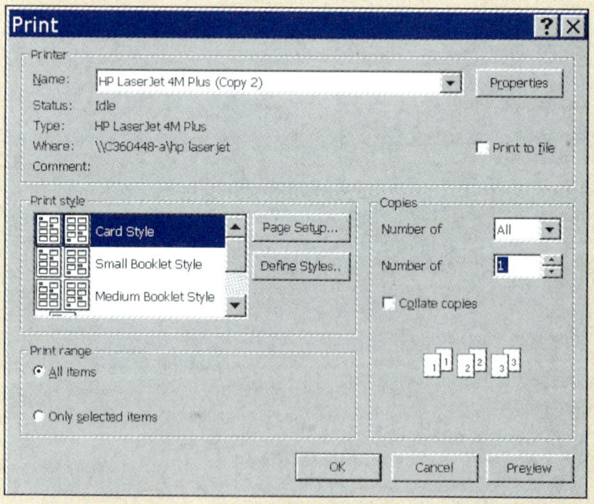

Figure 1.10
Print dialog box

2 SELECT: Card Style in the *Print style* list box, if it isn't selected already.

3 Ensure that *All items* is selected in the *Print range* area.

4 To preview how your contact list will appear when printed:
CLICK: Preview button in the Print dialog box
CLICK: Actual Size button (icon) in the Print Preview toolbar
Your screen should now appear similar, but not identical, to Figure 1.11.

Figure 1.11
Previewing your contact list

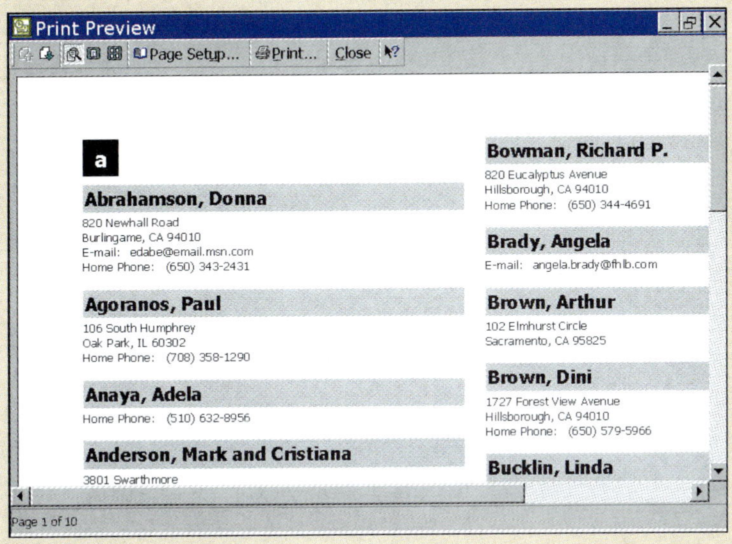

5 To further customize your contact-list printout:
CLICK: Page Setup button on the Print Preview toolbar
The Page Setup dialog box, shown in Figure 1.12, contains three tabs for customizing your final printout. You can use the *Format* tab to change your printout's font formatting and layout, and the *Paper* tab to select an alternate paper type, change margins, and apply a landscape orientation. The *Header/Footer* tab lets you specify what text you want to appear on the top or bottom of each page of your printout.

Figure 1.12
Page Setup dialog box

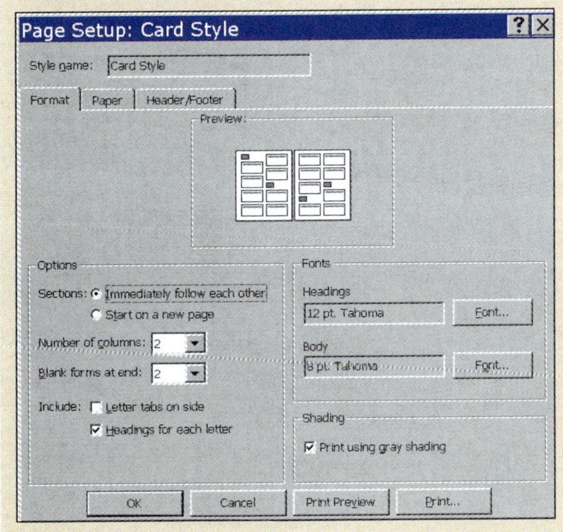

OUTLOOK

6. To leave the Page Setup dialog box without making any changes:
   CLICK: Cancel command button

7. To proceed with printing your contact list:
   CLICK: Print button on the Print Preview toolbar
   CLICK: OK command button

8. As a final step, let's delete the three practice contacts from your contact list.
   CLICK: Practice 1 contact item in the Information Viewer
   CLICK: Delete button (☒) on the Standard toolbar
   CLICK: Practice 2 contact item in the Information Viewer
   CLICK: Delete button (☒) on the Standard toolbar
   CLICK: Practice 3 contact item in the Information Viewer
   CLICK: Delete button (☒) on the Standard toolbar

1.2 Self Check By default, how is your contact list sorted into order?

1.3 Creating Reminder Notes

Many of us like to keep a good supply of sticky notes in our supply drawers for reminding us of details that might otherwise get past us. Outlook's Notes tool represents the electronic equivalent of an unlimited stack of sticky notes. You can create as many as you like and locate them with ease. In this module, you practice working with and managing note items.

1.3.1 Working with Note Items

FEATURE
A note is the only type of Outlook item that isn't presented in a dialog box with a Menu bar and toolbar. For this reason, note items are easier to use than other Outlook items.

METHOD
To create a note item:

1. CLICK: Notes icon ( ) in the Outlook Bar
2. CLICK: New Note button ( ) on the Standard toolbar and then type your note
3. To close a note item:
   CLICK: Close button ( ) in the note window, or
   CLICK: once in the Information Viewer area

To edit a note item:

1. CLICK: Notes icon ( ) in the Outlook Bar
2. DOUBLE-CLICK: your note

To view note items in different ways:

1. CLICK: Notes icon ( ) in the Outlook Bar
2. CHOOSE: View, Current View, *option*

PRACTICE
In this lesson, you practice creating, editing, and viewing note items.

Setup: Ensure that Outlook is loaded.

1 To access the Notes tool and create a note:
CLICK: Notes icon ( ) in the Outlook Bar
CLICK: New Note button ( ) on the Standard toolbar
The insertion point is blinking in a blank note that looks like a sticky note.

2. TYPE: **The exercises at the end of this chapter must be completed by Friday.**
Your note should now appear similar to the following:

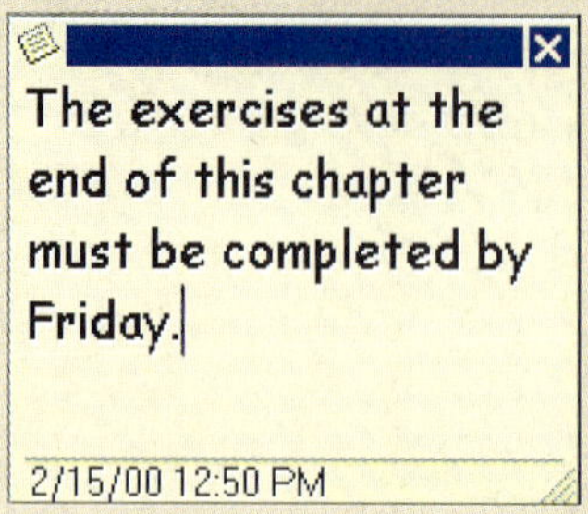

3. To close the note window:
CLICK: its Close button (☒)
You should now see the note item listed in the Information Viewer. If not, use the Information Viewer's scroll bars.

4. Let's edit the note you created and change the day from Friday to Thursday.
DOUBLE-CLICK: the note item in the Information Viewer
The note item should open into what looks like a sticky note.

5. SELECT: Friday in the note item
TYPE: **Thursday**

6. To display a menu of options related to your note:
CLICK: the note icon located in the upper-left corner of the note item
Your screen should now appear similar to Figure 1.13. You can use the note menu to perform several useful procedures with your note including save it to a separate document file, delete it, forward it to someone else via e-mail, move and copy text, change the note's color, and print the note.

Figure 1.13

Displaying a menu of note options

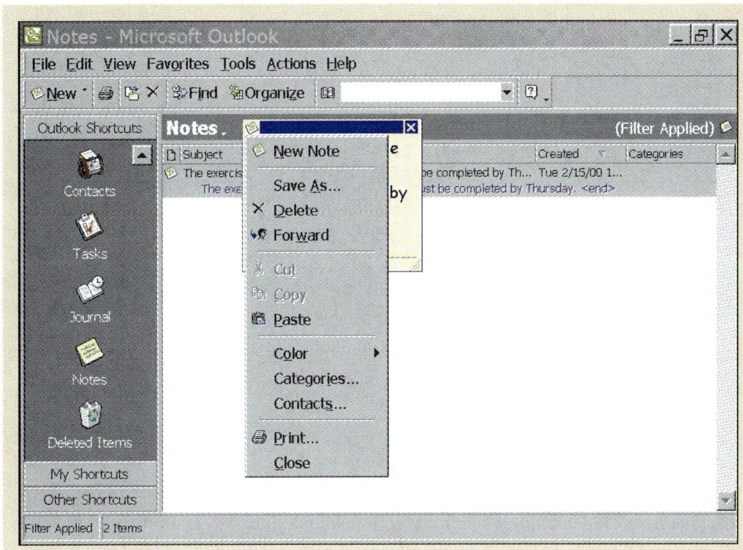

7. To leave the menu without making a selection:
CLICK: the note icon located in the upper-left corner of the note item again

8. This time, let's close the note item by clicking in the Information Viewer area.
CLICK: in the Information Viewer area

9. Another way to create a note is by pressing CTRL + SHIFT + **n** while using any Outlook tool. This way, you don't have to switch gears to record that important thought. To illustrate:
CLICK: Contacts icon ( ) in the Outlook Bar
PRESS: CTRL + SHIFT + **n**
A new note item should open.

10. TYPE: **Don't forget to pick up the laundry this afternoon.**
CLICK: the note item's Close button ( )
Although it seems as if the note item has disappeared into electronic never-never land, it is stored along with the rest of your notes.

11. CLICK: Notes icon ( ) in the Outlook Bar
You should see your note in the note list.

12. Let's display your notes list in a different format.
CHOOSE: View, Current View, Icons
The Information Viewer should now contain at least two icons, as shown below, representing your notes.

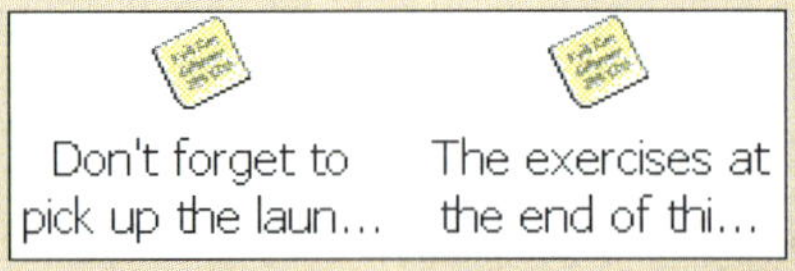

13 You can also organize your notes by color or when they were last created. To display all the notes you've created in the last seven days:
CHOOSE: View, Current View, Last Seven Days

14 To return your notes display to its original view:
CHOOSE: View, Current View, Notes List

1.3.2 Changing the Look of Your Notes

FEATURE
By default, note items are yellow and text displays using a 10-point Comic Sans MS font. You can easily change the look of new notes and of notes you've already created.

METHOD
To customize the appearance of new note items:

1. CHOOSE: Tools, Options
2. CLICK: *Preferences* tab
3. CLICK: Note Options command button
4. CLICK: OK command button after making your selections
5. CLICK: OK command button to close the Options dialog box

To change the color of an existing note:

1. DOUBLE-CLICK: the note item
2. CLICK: note icon in the upper-left corner of the note item
3. CHOOSE: Color, *color*

PRACTICE
In this lesson, you practice customizing note items.

Setup: Ensure that you've completed the previous lesson in this module and that your notes list is displaying.

1 Locate the note you created at the end of the previous lesson. This note reminds you to pick up your laundry.
DOUBLE-CLICK: note item about your laundry

2 To change the color of this note:
CLICK: note icon in the upper-left corner of the note item
CHOOSE: Color
CHOOSE: Pink
The note should now be pink.

3 CLICK: the note item's Close button (☒)

4 On your own, change the color of the first note you created in the previous lesson to the color of your choice.

5 Let's customize the appearance of new note items.
CHOOSE: Tools, Options to display the *Preferences* tab
CLICK: Note Options command button
The Notes Options dialog box should now appear (Figure 1.14).

Figure 1.14
Notes Options dialog box

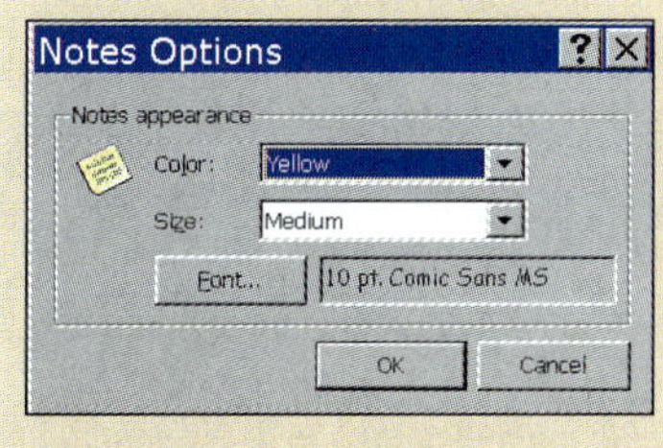

6 SELECT: Green from the *Color* drop-down list
SELECT: Large from the *Size* drop-down list

7 To change the font:
CLICK: Font command button
SELECT: Bold Italic from the *Font style* list box
SELECT: 12 from the *Size* list box
CLICK: OK command button

8 CLICK: OK command button to close the Notes Options dialog box
CLICK: OK command button to close the Options dialog box

9 Now let's create a new note to see the effect of our selections.
CLICK: New Note button (▣) on the Standard toolbar
TYPE: **Remember: Experience is what you get when you do not get what you want.**
Your note should appear similar to the following:

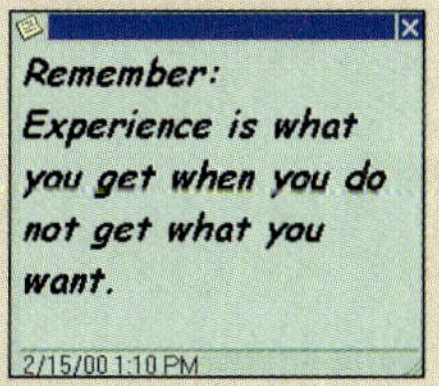

OUTLOOK

10. Close the note item.

11. On your own, use the Tools, Options command to display new note items using yellow, a medium size, and a regular, 10-point font.

12. As a final step in this lesson, delete the three notes you created in this and the previous lesson. To delete a note, click the note in the notes list and then click the Delete button (☒) on the Standard toolbar.

13. Before continuing, ensure that you've deleted the three notes you added in this and the previous lesson.

1.3 Self Check What is the Notes tool used for?

1.4 Getting Help

Outlook provides several **context-sensitive help** features and a comprehensive library of online documentation. Like many developers trying to minimize the retail price of software and maximize profits, Microsoft has stopped shipping volumes of print-based documentation in favor of disk-based Help systems. However, a Help system is only as good as the search tools that it provides. Fortunately for us, Windows gives developers the tools and capability to create consistent and easy-to-use Help systems. This section describes the context-sensitive help features found in Outlook and then describes where to find more detailed information using the Help window.

1.4.1 Obtaining Context-Sensitive Help

FEATURE
Context-sensitive help refers to a software program's ability to retrieve and present helpful information reflecting your current position in the program. In Outlook, you can access context-sensitive help for menu options and toolbar buttons. The help information is presented concisely in a small pop-up window that you can remove with the click of the mouse. This type of help lets you access information quickly and then continue working without interruption. Outlook also provides a special Help tool called the Office Assistant. The Office Assistant watches your keystrokes as you work and offers suggestions and shortcuts.

METHOD
To access help for menu options and toolbar buttons:

1. CHOOSE: Help, What's This? from the Menu bar
2. CHOOSE: desired command or click the desired button using the question mark mouse pointer

To display the Office Assistant:

- CHOOSE: Help, Show the Office Assistant, or
- CLICK: Microsoft Outlook Help button (?) on the Standard toolbar

PRACTICE
In this lesson, you access context-sensitive help information.

Setup: Ensure that Outlook is loaded.

1 In the next few steps, you practice choosing Help, What's This? to access Help for the File, New command and one of the toolbar buttons. Let's start with the File, New command.
CHOOSE: Help, What's This?
The question mark mouse pointer is now activated.

2 CHOOSE: File, New, Appointment
Rather than executing the command, Outlook provides a description of the command.

3 After reading the description, close the window by clicking on it once.

4 To display information about a toolbar button:
CHOOSE: Help, What's This?
CLICK: Print button (🖨) on the Standard toolbar

The following pop-up window appears:

> **Print (File menu)**
>
> Prints the active file or selected items. To select print options, click the **File** menu, and then click **Print.**

5 CLICK: the pop-up window once to remove it

6 Now let's display the Office Assistant.
CHOOSE: Help

7 Perform one of the following two procedures, depending on what you see in the Help menu:

a. If the "Hide the Office Assistant" option appears in the Help menu, then the Office Assistant is already working for you even though you don't currently see it. To display the Office Assistant:
CLICK: Microsoft Outlook Help button ( ) on the Standard toolbar

b. If the "Show the Office Assistant" option appears in the Help menu, then the Office Assistant isn't currently working for you. To activate and display the Office Assistant:
CHOOSE: Show the Office Assistant

The Office Assistant may appear as a paperclip (by default) or as another character. The Office Assistant and its associated tip window should now appear. (*Note:* If a tip window doesn't appear, click the Office Assistant character once.)

8 To find out more about obtaining help information in Outlook, do the following:
TYPE: **How do I obtain help in Outlook?**
PRESS: ENTER
The Office Assistant and associated tip window should appear similar to Figure 1.15. Each of the topics in the tip window is a link to corresponding help information.

Figure 1.15
Office Assistant and tip window

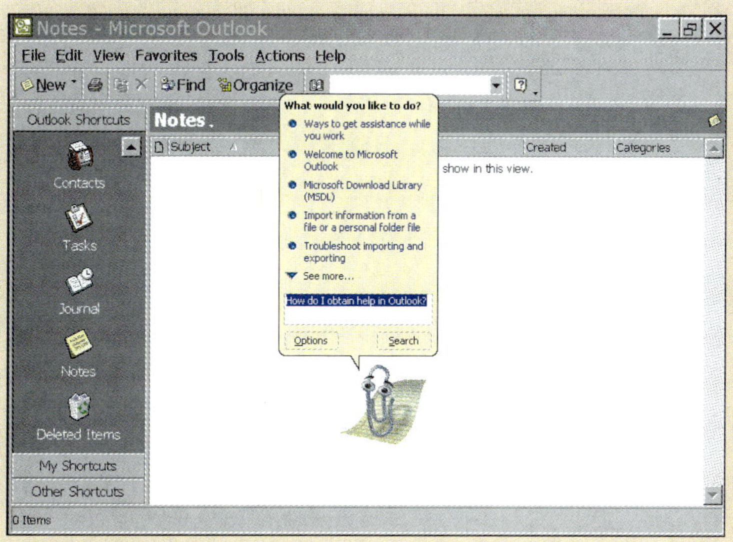

9 In the tip window:
CLICK: "Ways to get assistance while you work" link
The information you've requested will appear in a Help window.

10 Ensure that the Help window is maximized. (*Note:* We describe the Help window in the next lesson.) Your screen should now appear similar to Figure 1.16.

Figure 1.16
Displaying information about your selected topic

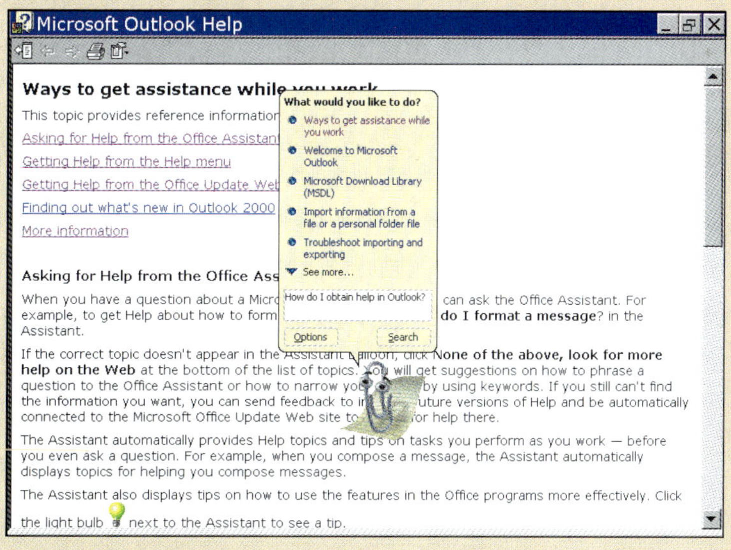

11 To close the Help window:
CLICK: the window's Close button (☒)

12 The Office Assistant character, without the tip window, appears on your screen. When the Office Assistant is displaying, it will watch your keystrokes and display relevant help information in its tip window. To illustrate:
CHOOSE: File, Import and Export
The Office Assistant is now displaying a tip window asking if you would like help with this procedure.

13 To close the Import and Export Wizard dialog box:
CLICK: Cancel command button
The tip window no longer appears. Occasionally an illuminated lightbulb will appear in the Office Assistant box. This is the Office Assistant's way of telling you it has a new tip or suggestion. You tell the Office Assistant that you want to view the tip by clicking the lightbulb.

14 To remove the Office Assistant from display:
CHOOSE: Help, Hide the Office Assistant

1.4.2 Using the Help Window

FEATURE

Another way to access help information in Outlook is to use the Help window. You can think of the Help window as the front door to Outlook's vast help resources. The Help window provides three different tools, each on its own tab, to help you find the information you need quickly and easily. The *Contents* tab displays a list of help topics organized as a hierarchy of books and pages. Think of this tab as the Table of Contents for the entire Help system. The *Answer Wizard* tab lets you obtain answers by typing in words and phrases. The *Index* tab displays an alphabetical list of keywords and phrases, similar to a traditional book index. To search for a topic using this tab, you type a word (or even a few letters) into the text box which, in turn, makes the list box scroll to the first matching entry in the index.

METHOD

1. Ensure that the Office Assistant is turned off.
2. CHOOSE: Help, Microsoft Outlook Help from the Menu bar, or CLICK: Microsoft Outlook Help button (?) on the Standard toolbar

PRACTICE
In this lesson, you turn off the Office Assistant and then display the Help window.

Setup: Ensure that Outlook is loaded and that you completed the previous lesson. Although the Office Assistant isn't displaying, it is still activated.

1. CLICK: Microsoft Outlook Help button ( )
The Office Assistant and associated tip window should appear. Let's deactivate the Office Assistant so that the Help window will display when we click the Microsoft Outlook Help button ( ).

2. CLICK: Options button in the tip window
The Office Assistant dialog box will now appear (Figure 1.17).

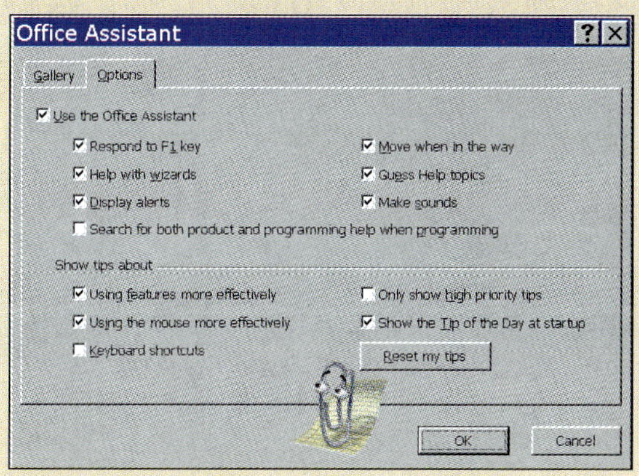

Figure 1.17
Office Assistant dialog box: *Options* tab

3. To deactivate the Office Assistant:
CLICK: *Use the Office Assistant* check box to deselect it
CLICK: OK command button

4. Now, let's see what happens when we access help.
CLICK: Microsoft Outlook Help button ( )
CLICK: Maximize button ( ) in the Help window's Title bar
Your screen should now appear similar to Figure 1.18.

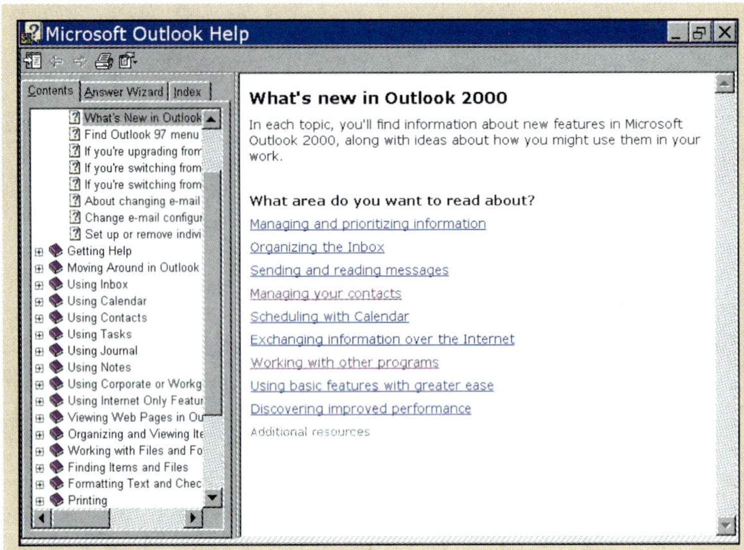

Figure 1.18
Displaying the Help window

5. If your display doesn't show the three tabs located on the left side of the screen, do the following:
CLICK: Options button (▣) on the toolbar
CHOOSE: Show Tabs
CLICK: *Contents* tab
Your screen should now appear similar to Figure 1.18.

6. To display the contents of a topic:
DOUBLE-CLICK: "Moving Around in Outlook" topic
This particular topic contains five additional topic pages and three topic categories.

7. To further refine the search:
DOUBLE-CLICK: "Using the Outlook Bar" category
Note that this book contains multiple topic pages.

8. To display a topic page:
CLICK: "Show or hide the Outlook Bar" topic
Information about the topic appears in the frame to the right.

9. To close the current topic category:
DOUBLE-CLICK: "Using the Outlook Bar" category
Note that the list of books and topics is collapsed under the book icon.

10. Let's search for some information using the keyword index:
CLICK: *Index* tab

11. To find topics related to Outlook's Contacts feature:
TYPE: **contact**
The keywords list located below automatically scrolls to highlight "contact."

12 In the keyword list:
DOUBLE-CLICK: contact
A list of topics appears in the *Choose a topic* list box. Information about the currently selected topic appears in the frame to the right.

13 In the *Choose a topic* list box:
DOUBLE-CLICK: "About Contacts"
The resulting information appears in the frame to the right.

14 To print the current topic:
CLICK: Print button (🖶) on the toolbar
CLICK: OK command button to print the entire topic

15 Let's close the Help window. To do so:
CLICK: Close button (☒) in the window's Title bar

1.4 Self Check What is context-sensitive help?

1.5 Chapter Review

Microsoft Outlook is used for managing your most important resource—information. Once Outlook is loaded, you can access its tools by clicking their corresponding icons in the Outlook Bar. This chapter focused on using the Contacts tool for collecting and managing contact information, and the Notes tool for displaying reminder notes. You also learned how to display context-sensitive help information and to use Outlook's Help window.

1.5.1 Command Summary

Many of the commands and procedures appearing in this chapter are summarized in the following table.

Skill Set	To Perform This Task . . .	Do the Following . . .
Navigating and Using Outlook 2000 Effectively	Navigate among Outlook's components	CLICK: group button to display its contents CLICK: desired shortcut icon
	Change the size of icons in the Outlook Bar	RIGHT-CLICK: the background of the Outlook Bar CHOOSE: Large Icons or Small Icons
	Switch Outlook views	CLICK: tool icon in the Outlook Bar CHOOSE: View, Current View, *option*
	Access help for menu options and toolbar buttons	CHOOSE: Help, What's This?
	Display the Office Assistant	CHOOSE: Help, Show the Office Assistant, or CLICK: Microsoft Outlook Help button (?) on the Standard toolbar
	Display the Help window	1. Ensure that the Office Assistant is turned off. 2. CHOOSE: Help, Microsoft Outlook Help from the Menu bar, or CLICK: Microsoft Outlook Help button (?) on the Standard toolbar
Using Contacts	Add a contact item	CLICK: Contacts icon ( ) in the Outlook Bar CLICK: New Contact button ( )
	Edit a contact item	DOUBLE-CLICK: a contact item

Continued

Skill Set	To Perform This Task . . .	Do the Following . . .
Using Contacts *Continued*	Delete a contact item	CLICK: the contact item in the Information Viewer to select it CLICK: Delete button (☒) on the Standard toolbar
	Sort a contact list	CHOOSE: View, Current View, Customize Current View CLICK: Sort command button
	Print a contact list	CHOOSE: File, Print, or CLICK: Print button (🖶) on the Standard toolbar
	Manually record a contact activity in Journal	1. Open the contact item or select it in the Information Viewer. 2. CHOOSE: Actions, New Journal Entry for Contact
Using Notes	Create a note item	CLICK: Notes icon ( ) in the Outlook Bar CLICK: New Note button ( )
	Edit a note item	DOUBLE-CLICK: a note item
	View your notes as icons	CLICK: Notes icon ( ) in the Outlook Bar CHOOSE: View, Current View, Icons
	Organize note items	CLICK: Notes icon ( ) in the Outlook Bar CHOOSE: View, Current View CHOOSE: Last Seven Days, By Category, or By Color from the menu
	Change the color of an existing note	DOUBLE-CLICK: the note item CLICK: note icon in the upper-left corner of the note item CHOOSE: Color, *color*
	Customize the appearance of new notes	CHOOSE: Tools, Options CLICK: *Preferences* tab CLICK: Note Options command button

1.5.2 Key Terms

This section specifies page references for the key terms identified in this chapter. For a complete list of definitions, refer to the Glossary provided immediately after the Appendix in this learning guide.

Calendar, *p. 3*

Contacts, *p. 3*

context-sensitive help, *p. 28*

Inbox, *p. 3*

Journal, *p. 4*

Microsoft Outlook 2000, *p. 3*

Notes, *p. 4*

Outlook Today, *p. 3*

Tasks, *p. 3*

1.6 Review Questions

1.6.1 Short Answer

1. What is the procedure for printing a list of contacts?
2. What is the procedure for sorting a list of contacts?
3. How can you change the current view in Outlook?
4. In what ways can you customize the Outlook Today tool?
5. What is the procedure for deactivating the Office Assistant?
6. In the Help window, how is the *Contents* tab used?
7. What is Outlook Today used for?
8. In what ways can you change the appearance of note items?
9. What is the procedure for accessing help for menu options and toolbar buttons?
10. What is the procedure for deleting a note from your notes list?

1.6.2 True/False

1. ____ It's possible to customize the Outlook Today tool so that it doesn't display at startup.
2. ____ The Notes tool lets you keep track of tasks that need to be performed, including their priority.
3. ____ A Contacts folder can't contain more than 150 names and addresses.
4. ____ Inbox provides a tool for organizing appointments.
5. ____ To access the command for customizing Notes, choose Tools, Options from the Menu bar.
6. ____ To edit a contact item, simply click it once.
7. ____ It's possible to print a contact list in a variety of formats.

8. ____ You can use the Contacts tool to keep track of a person's birthday.
9. ____ To switch among tools using the Outlook bar, you simply click the tool's icon.
10. ____ It's possible to change the size of the icons in the Outlook Bar.

1.6.3 Multiple Choice

1. Which of the following tools should you use to maintain a list of addresses?
   a. Inbox
   b. Calendar
   c. Contacts
   d. Journal

2. Which of the following tools would you use to compose an e-mail message about an upcoming appointment?
   a. Inbox
   b. Calendar
   c. Contacts
   d. Journal

3. Which of the following tools records when events take place on a single timeline?
   a. Inbox
   b. Calendar
   c. Contacts
   d. Journal

4. To access a tool in the Outlook Bar, you must:
   a. click its icon once
   b. double-click its icon
   c. right-click its icon
   d. CHOOSE: Tools, Open

5. Is it possible to change the current view of each one of the Outlook tools?
   a. yes
   b. no
   c. usually
   d. yes, except for Inbox

6. Which of the following isn't an Outlook tool?
   a. Calendar
   b. Journal
   c. Notes
   d. To Do List

7. Journal provides a tool for keeping track of activities such as:
   a. phone calls
   b. e-mail messages
   c. notes
   d. all of the above

8. Outlook refers to the information it manages, such as an e-mail message or address, as __________.
   a. objects
   b. items
   c. things
   d. all of the above

9. When adding a contact, which of the following tabs would you use to store a person's nickname?
   a. *General* tab
   b. *Details* tab
   c. *Activities* tab
   d. none of the above

10. By default, contact items are sorted by the __________ field.
   a. Last Name
   b. Zip Code
   c. File As
   d. Area Code

1.7 Hands-On Projects

1.7.1 Creative Design Picture Framing: Touring Outlook

This exercise practices loading Outlook, navigating among and comparing Outlook's components, changing the size of the Outlook Bar icons, and customizing and printing the Outlook Today folder.

1. Load Outlook from the Quick Launch toolbar and then maximize the Outlook application window, if necessary.

2. To display the Outlook Today screen in the Information Viewer:
   CLICK: Outlook Shortcuts group button in the Outlook Bar
   CLICK: Outlook Today icon ( ) in the Outlook Bar

3. Let's compare the Standard toolbars of the Tasks and Notes tools:
CLICK: Tasks icon () in the Outlook Bar and observe the Standard toolbar
CLICK: Notes icon () in the Outlook Bar and note how the Standard toolbar has changed

4. Now let's observe the differences between the menu items of the Inbox and Calendar tools:
CLICK: Inbox icon () in the Outlook Bar
CHOOSE: Actions menu command and observe the available options from the pull-down menu
CLICK: Calendar icon () in the Outlook Bar
CHOOSE: Actions menu command and note how the menu options have changed

5. To display small icons in the Other Shortcuts group of the Outlook Bar:
CLICK: Other Shortcuts group button in the Outlook Bar
RIGHT-CLICK: in the background of the Outlook Bar
CHOOSE: Small Icons from the right-click menu

6. Let's change the appearance of the Outlook Today folder. To ensure the contents of the Outlook Today folder are displaying in the Information Viewer:
CLICK: Outlook Shortcuts group button
CLICK: Outlook Today icon () in the Outlook Bar

7. To customize the Outlook Today folder to use the Standard style in a single column:
CLICK: Customize Outlook Today hyperlink
CLICK: drop-down arrow in the *Styles* area
CHOOSE: Standard (one column) from the drop-down list
CLICK: Save Changes hyperlink

8. To print the customized Outlook Today folder:
CHOOSE: File, Print
CLICK: OK command button

9. To return the Other Shortcuts icons in the Outlook Bar to large icons:
CLICK: Other Shortcuts group button in the Outlook Bar
RIGHT-CLICK: in the background of the Outlook Bar
CHOOSE: Large Icons

10. Finally, to return the Outlook Today folder to the standard style:
    CLICK: Customize Outlook Today hyperlink
    CLICK: drop-down arrow in the *Styles* area
    CHOOSE: Standard from the drop-down list
    CLICK: Save Changes hyperlink to return the Outlook Today folder to its original appearance

1.7.2 Summit Career College: Using the Contacts Tool

In this exercise, you use the Contacts tool to add and edit contact items, compare several contact list views, and print the contact list.

1. Let's add information about a new professor to your contact list:
   CLICK: Outlook Shortcuts group button in the Outlook Bar
   CLICK: Contacts icon ( ) in the Outlook Bar
   CLICK: New Contact button ( ) on the Standard toolbar to produce the Contact window
2. To enter the professor's name directly into the *Full Name* text box:
   CLICK: in the *Full Name* text box
   TYPE: **Dorothy Wizard**
3. To add the professor's remaining name information:
   PRESS: TAB to move the insertion point to the *Job title* text box
   TYPE: **Professor**
   PRESS: TAB to move the insertion point to the *Company* text box
   TYPE: **Ozborne College**
4. To change how Professor Wizard's name is filed:
   CLICK: *File as* drop-down arrow
   SELECT: Wizard, Dorothy (Ozborne College) from the *File as* drop-down list
5. To add Professor Wizard's address information using a structured form:
   CLICK: Address command button
   TYPE: **333 Toto Drive** in the *Street* text box
   PRESS: TAB to move to the *City* text box
   TYPE: **Kansas City**
   PRESS: TAB to move to the *State/Province* text box
   TYPE: **Oklahoma**
   PRESS: TAB to move to the *Zip/Postal Code* text box
   TYPE: **74988**

6. To complete the dialog box:
CLICK: *Country/Region* drop-down arrow
SELECT: United States of America
CLICK: OK command button
7. To save Professor Wizard's contact information:
CLICK: Save and Close button on the Standard toolbar
8. Let's edit Professor Wizard's contact information.
DOUBLE-CLICK: Professor Wizard's contact item
CLICK: *Details* tab
CLICK: *Birthday* drop-down arrow
CLICK: Today command button from the drop-down calendar
CLICK: Save and Close button
9. Let's add one more professor to the contact database:
CLICK: New Contact button (icon) on the Standard toolbar
CLICK: Full Name command button
CLICK: *Title* drop-down arrow
SELECT: Prof. from the *Title* drop-down list
CLICK: in the *First* text box
TYPE: **Wanda**
CLICK: in the *Last* text box
TYPE: **West**
CLICK: OK command button
10. To add Professor West's Company information:
CLICK: in the *Company* text box
TYPE: **Washington State University**
11. Let's enter Professor West's address directly in the *Address* text box:
CLICK: in the *Address* text box
TYPE: **787 Witch Way**
PRESS: ENTER
TYPE: **Wickedton, Washington 76543**
12. To add a reminder to yourself about Professor West:
CLICK: in the large text box on the bottom of the form
TYPE: **Wanda is the Wicked Witch of the West!**
CLICK: Save and Close button
13. Let's compare several contact list views:
CHOOSE: View, Current View, By Company
CHOOSE: View, Current View, By Location
CHOOSE: View, Current View, Detailed Address Cards
14. To print the contact list:
CHOOSE: View, Current View, Detailed Address Cards (if not already selected)
CHOOSE: File, Print
SELECT: Card Style in the *Print Style* list box (if not already selected)
CLICK: OK command button

15. After successfully printing the contact list, remove Professor Wizard's and Professor West's information from your contact database:
    CLICK: Professor Wizard contact item in the Information Viewer
    CLICK: Delete button (☒) on the Standard toolbar
    CLICK: Professor West contact item in the Information Viewer
    CLICK: Delete button (☒) on the Standard toolbar

1.7.3 Rapunzel's Hair Design: Using the Notes Tool

You will now practice creating, editing, customizing, viewing, and printing note items.

1. Display the Notes tool in the Information Viewer.
2. Create a new note using the New Note button ( ) on the Standard toolbar.
3. Type the following information in the new note:
   Tell Tanya that Mrs. Jacobs has canceled her appointment for today.
4. Change the note's color to blue.
5. Create a new note by pressing CTRL + SHIFT + **n** rather than using the toolbar button.
6. Type the following text in the new note:
   Order more Shimmer Shampoo from Leon!
7. Change all future new note items to be pink and large sized, and to display text in a bold, italic, Arial font.
8. Create a new note with the following message:
   Donna and Tanya's scissors need to be sharpened.
9. Edit the blue note to read "Frank" rather than "Leon."
10. Display all of your notes using the Notes List view.
11. Print your notes list using the Table Style, ensuring *All rows* has been selected in the *Print range* area.
12. After successfully printing, change the appearance of all future note items to yellow and their size to medium. Also, change the appearance of note text to a 10-point size and a Comic Sans MS font.

1.7.4 Armstrong Equipment Rental: Accessing Outlook Help

You will now practice accessing and printing help information using the Help window and by accessing context-sensitive help.

1. Use the "What's This?" command from the Help menu to display a description of the Favorites, Add to Favorites menu command.
2. Close the description window.
3. Use the "What's This?" command to display information about the New button on the Standard toolbar.
4. Remove the pop-up window.
5. Use the Office Assistant to ask the following question: **How do you delete a note?**
6. Deactivate the Office Assistant.
7. Open and maximize the Microsoft Outlook Help window.
8. Use the *Contents* tab to open the "Using Notes" category and to display the "About Notes" topic page.
9. Print the "About Notes" topic page.
10. Close the Help window.

1.7.5 On Your Own: Creating a Contact List

Using the Contacts tool, add four fictitious or real contacts to your contact list. Provide as much information as possible, using both the *General* and *Details* tabs. For each of your contacts, complete the *File as* text box by typing either *Friend* or *Family* on the *General* tab. View the completed contact list using the following three views: Detailed Address Cards, Phone List, and By Location. Sort your contact listing into ascending order by the State field. Then, print your contact list using the Table style.

1.7.6 On Your Own: Creating Reminder Notes

As the receptionist at the Amber Chiropractic and Massage Therapy Clinic, use the Notes tool to create four different reminders to yourself. Customize each of the notes by changing their color, size, and font. Practice editing the notes and then displaying them using four different views. Finally, print a copy of your favorite note.

1.8 Case Problems: SilverHome Accommodation

Now that Narissa and Stan have Outlook 2000 installed on their computer, they are eager to put it to work. They look forward to more easily managing contact information for their vacation rental customers from around the world, their housecleaning staff, and their maintenance personnel. And they hope Outlook will rescue them from constantly misplaced messages and reminders.

In the following case problems, assume the roles of Stan and Narissa Byron and perform the same steps that they identify. You may want to re-read the chapter opening before proceeding.

1. Since Narissa hasn't had a chance to work with Outlook yet, Stan decides to give her a brief tour. He loads Microsoft Outlook 2000 from the Start button and shows Narissa where the Title bar, Menu bar, Standard toolbar, Outlook Bar, and Information Viewer are located in the application window. He then shows her how to display the icons in the My Shortcuts group of the Outlook Bar as small icons. Next, he redisplays them using large icons.

   To coordinate with their current winter ski season, Stan decides to customize their Outlook Today folder with the Winter style. He then prints a copy of the Outlook Today folder for Narissa. After printing, Stan and Narissa decide to reapply the Standard style to the Outlook Today folder.

2. After guiding Narissa around Outlook, he decides to show her how to use the Contacts tool. Before long, Narissa takes over the controls and adds the following business names, titles, company names, and addresses to their contact list:

Miss Elaine Thiessen
Job Title: **Housecleaning Manager**
Company: **Maid to Klean Company**
Address: **403 Notch Hill Road**
Vernon, British Columbia
V1B 4R4 Canada

Jonathan David Schuler Jr.
Job Title: **Plumber**
Company: **Schuler & Sons Plumbing Ltd.**
Address: **Box 24**
Kelowna, British Columbia
V4T 3W3 Canada

Dr. Raymond E. Madison
Job Title: **Veterinarian**
Company: **Sunridge Veterinary Clinic**
Address: **Suite 101, 2899 – 30 Street**
Vernon, British Columbia
V1B 1Q8 Canada

Stan reminds Narissa to add phone numbers to their contact list. Narissa edits each contact by adding the following:

- Elaine's Business phone number (**250-549-8888**)
- Jonathan's Business phone number (**250-861-2222**)
- Jonathan's Home phone number (**250-861-3333**)
- Dr. Madison's Business phone number (**250-545-6666**)

Narissa suddenly remembers that Elaine's birthday is on October 7, and that Jonathan's nickname is Johnny. Accordingly, she edits the contact list to include this additional information.

3. Stan decides to customize the appearance of their address listing. He views their contact list using the Address Cards view and then using the Detailed Address Cards view. He then customizes the contact list view to be sorted into ascending order by the Business Phone number. Finally, he prints a copy of the contact list. Using the Print command, he selects the Phone Directory Style and selects to print all items. Prior to printing, he previews the contact list.

4. As Stan is typing a letter at the computer, he receives a long distance phone call from a customer in Australia who would like to book the Silver Summit Chalet during the upcoming Christmas holiday. With no pen and paper nearby, Stan quickly opens Outlook's Notes tool and creates a new note. He types the customer's name (**Mr. Robert Bigelow**) and phone number (**613-488-9999**), and the required rental dates (**Dec. 21-30**).

   After terminating the phone conversation, Stan creates a new note using the appropriate keyboard shortcut. He addresses the note to Narissa asking her to check the availability of the Silver Summit Chalet over the Christmas season. Knowing that Narissa's favorite color is green, he changes this note's color to green. To practice printing Narissa's note, he selects the Memo Style in the Print dialog box and then sends the note to the printer.

NOTES

NOTES

MICROSOFT OUTLOOK 2000

Managing Everyday Information

CHAPTER TWO

Chapter Outline

Learning Objectives

After reading this chapter, you will be able to:

- Manage your appointment schedule
- Organize your task list
- Categorize Outlook items and create new folders for keeping your information organized
- Streamline Word's Menu bar and toolbars to your specific work habits and patterns

Case Study

Furniture Source

Based in Sheridan, Indiana, Furniture Source is a mail-order furniture and home accessories company that has been in business since 1986. The brainchild of Alphonso Banks, the company's president, Furniture Source provides a broad selection of quality products at prices that undercut most retail department stores. For the first four years of business, Mr. Banks marketed only to Indiana residents by means of a low-budget product catalog. In 1990, Mr. Banks decided to go national and build upon his successes in Indiana. He published a 70-page color catalog and distributed it to 500,000 homes throughout the United States. The market responded favorably and sales boomed. Today, with a distribution list of over 2 million, Furniture Source is an extremely successful, privately held company.

Kristen Grady has worked in many capacities at Furniture Source since 1992. Previously a telephone sales representative, Kristen was recently promoted to senior sales representative for the western region. Given her increased responsibilities, Kristen wants to tidy up her desk once and for all. Her desktop is buried in paper notes and her appointment calendar and address book are both covered with illegible scribbles. So that important details don't get past her, she has decided to begin using Microsoft Outlook.

In this chapter, you and Kristen learn how to use Outlook's Calendar tool to schedule appointments, events, and meetings. You will use the Tasks tool to create and manage tasks, and you will become more organized by working with categories, folders, and the Office Clipboard. Finally, you will customize your workspace by manipulating and customizing toolbars.

2.1 Managing Your Calendar

Since you've already seen lots of calendars in your lifetime, Outlook's calendar won't be a mystery to you. Like its paper counterpart, Outlook's electronic calendar is composed of rows and columns, the intersection of which represent the days of the week. You can use the Calendar tool to store appointment information, reminder notes, and even recurring events such as birthdays. You can even forward calendar information to others via e-mail. This tool is so intuitive to use that you can probably use it the first time without help from us. However, we would like to use this module to introduce you to some of its finer points.

2.1.1 Viewing Your Calendar

FEATURE
A nice feature of Outlook's electronic calendar is that you can view it in different ways. For example, you can view an entire month at once or view a particular day close up. You can also change the look of your calendar by selecting an alternate background color and workweek. You can further customize your calendar by importing your country's holidays and changing the current time zone.

METHOD
To view your calendar:

- CLICK: Go to Today button, Day button, Week button, or Month button on the Standard toolbar
- CHOOSE: View, Current View, *option* from the Menu bar

To customize your calendar:

1. CHOOSE: Tools, Options
2. CLICK: Calendar Options command button

PRACTICE
This lesson leads you through displaying your calendar in different ways and through customizing your calendar.

Setup: Ensure that Outlook is loaded.

1 To access the Calendar tool:
CLICK: Calendar icon ( ) in the Outlook Bar

2 To display today's date:
CLICK: Go to Today button on the Standard toolbar
This action selects the current date.

3 To view your calendar in Day view:
CLICK: Day button ( ) on the Standard toolbar
The Information Viewer area is now divided into three areas, each of which appears labeled in Figure 2.1. The Appointment area lists your day in 30-minute time slots. You can enter appointments directly into this area. To display a different date in the Appointment area, select the date using the Date Navigator. The TaskPad area displays your current task list by referring to information stored in your Tasks folder.

Figure 2.1
Viewing a day at a time

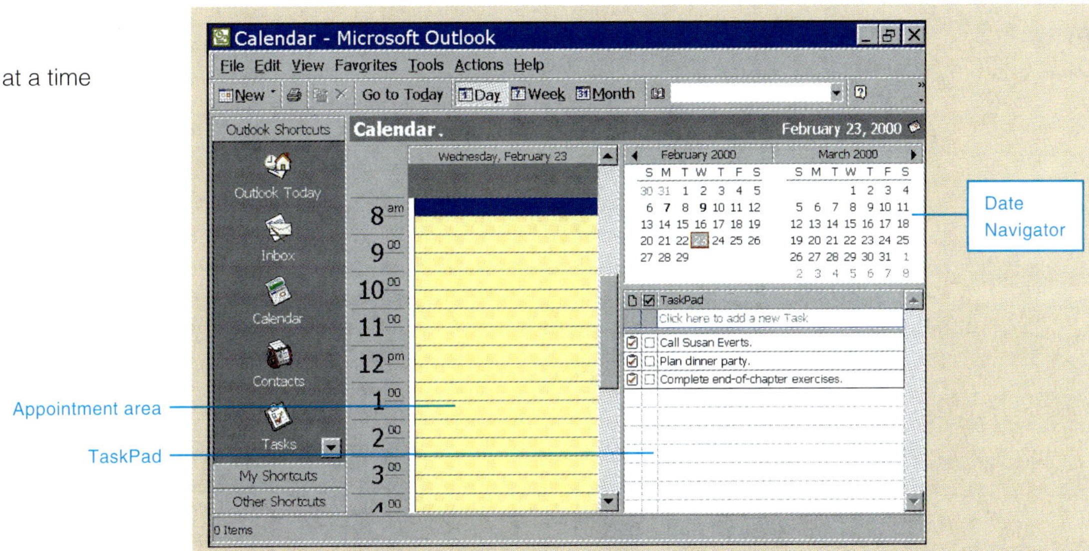

4 To glance at the current week:
CLICK: Week button on the Standard toolbar
Your screen should now appear similar, but not identical, to Figure 2.2.

Figure 2.2
Viewing a week at a time

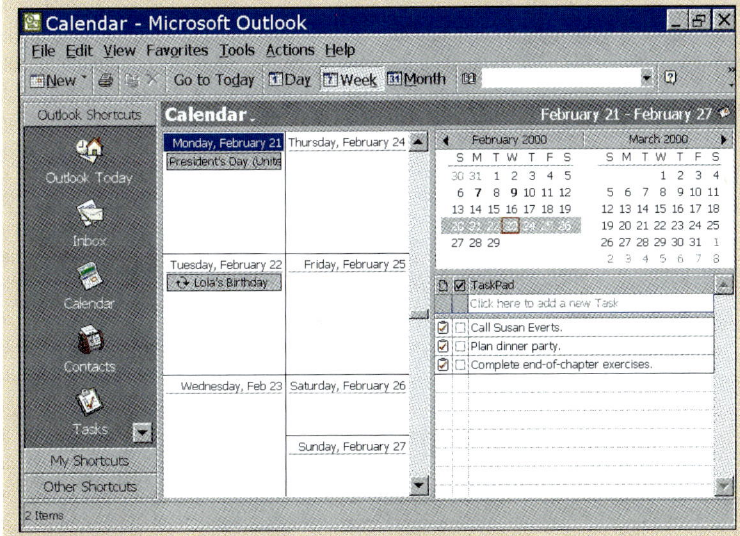

5 To view a month at a glance:
CLICK: Month button (31)
Your screen should now appear similar, but not identical, to Figure 2.3.

OUTLOOK

Figure 2.3

Viewing a month at a time

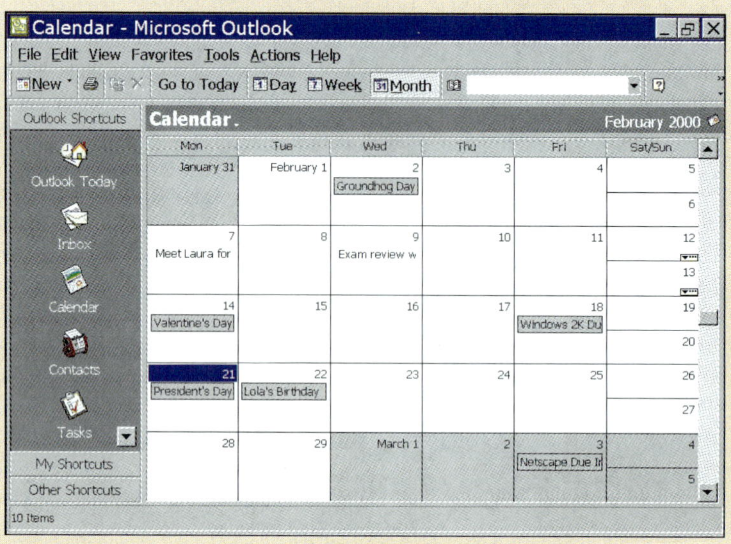

6 Let's look at how you can customize your calendar.
CHOOSE: Tools, Options
CLICK: Calendar Options command button
Your screen should now appear similar to Figure 2.4.

Figure 2.4

Calendar Options dialog box

Using this area, you can change the days and hours that compose your work week.

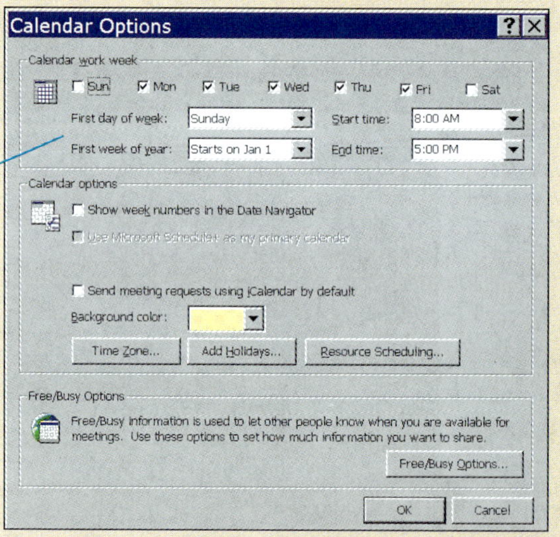

7 To return to your calendar without making any changes:
CLICK: OK command button to leave the Calendar Options dialog box
CLICK: OK command button to leave the Options dialog box

8 Continue to the next lesson.

2.1.2 Scheduling Appointments and Events

FEATURE

Although it's very easy to schedule appointments and events using a paper date book, scheduling in Outlook provides some distinct advantages. Outlook enables you to quickly schedule recurring appointments, such as monthly staff meetings, and multi-day events, such as offsite meetings. You can also sound a reminder when an appointment or event is about to occur. An *appointment* in Outlook takes place on a particular day and has a start and an end time. *Events* don't have start and end times. That is, although they may occur on a particular day, as is the case with birthdays, scheduling them doesn't mean you can't also schedule appointments and other events on the same day.

METHOD

To schedule an appointment:

1. CLICK: Calendar icon ( ) in the Outlook Bar
2. CLICK: New Appointment button ( ) on the Standard toolbar, or
   CHOOSE: Actions, New Appointment
3. At a minimum, provide information in the *Subject* text box, and *Start time* and *End time* drop-down lists.
4. Review the settings in the *Reminder* area.
5. If your appointment occurs every day, week, month, or year:
   CLICK: Recurrence button on the Standard toolbar
   CLICK: OK command button after providing information about your appointment's recurrence
6. CLICK: Save and Close on the Standard toolbar

To schedule an event:

1. CLICK: Calendar icon ( ) in the Outlook Bar
2. CHOOSE: Actions, New All Day Event
3. At a minimum, provide information in the *Subject* text box, and *Start time* and *End time* drop-down lists.
4. Review the settings in the *Reminder* area.
5. CLICK: Save and Close on the Standard toolbar

PRACTICE

This lesson practices scheduling appointments and events.

Setup: Ensure that you've completed the previous lesson and that you're viewing your calendar using the Month view.

1. To add an appointment describing an upcoming study session with a group of other students:
CLICK: New Appointment button (▣) on the Standard toolbar
The Appointment window opens.

2. Ensure that the Appointment window is maximized. Your screen should now appear similar to Figure 2.5.

Figure 2.5
The Appointment window

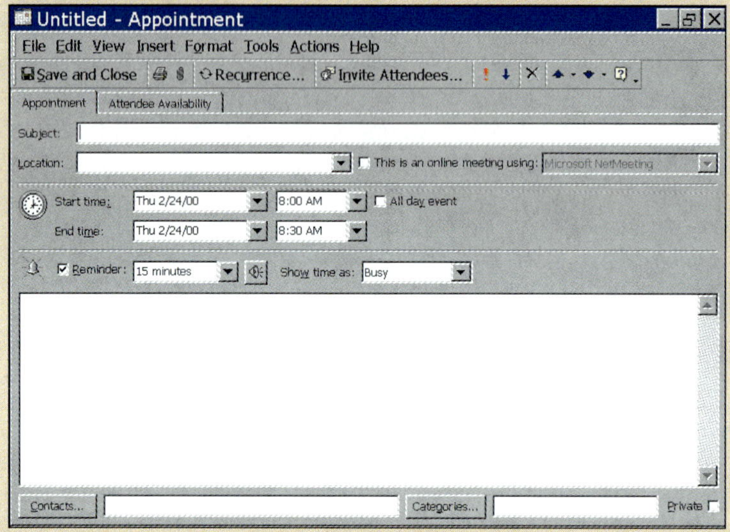

3. The insertion point is blinking in the *Subject* text box.
TYPE: **Study Session**

4. To schedule your study session:
CLICK: down arrow next to the date in the *Start time* area
CHOOSE: *a day that is one week from today*
(*Note:* You can also type in the date directly.)

5. To specify the time of the appointment using a drop-down list:
CLICK: down arrow next to the time in the *Start time* area
CHOOSE: 11:00 AM from the drop-down list

6. In the *End time* drop-down list of times, choose 2:00 PM. (You've just set aside three hours to study next week!)

7. Review the settings in the *Reminder* area. By default, Outlook reminds you of upcoming appointments 15 minutes before they're scheduled to occur. You can change this setting using the *Reminder* drop-down list. You can also select not to be reminded by deselecting the *Reminder* check box. (*Note:* You can change the reminder settings for all new appointments by first closing the current appointment window, choosing Tools, Options, and then editing the *Default reminder* settings.)

8 To save this appointment:
CLICK: Save and Close button on the Standard toolbar
The appointment should now be displaying in your calendar.

9 Let's edit your Study Session appointment so that it is scheduled as a weekly (recurring) appointment.
DOUBLE-CLICK: "Study Session" appointment item in your calendar
The details of your appointment should appear in the Appointment window.

10 CLICK: Recurrence button ( ) in the Standard toolbar
The Appointment Recurrence dialog box appears (Figure 2.6).

Figure 2.6
The Appointment Recurrence dialog box

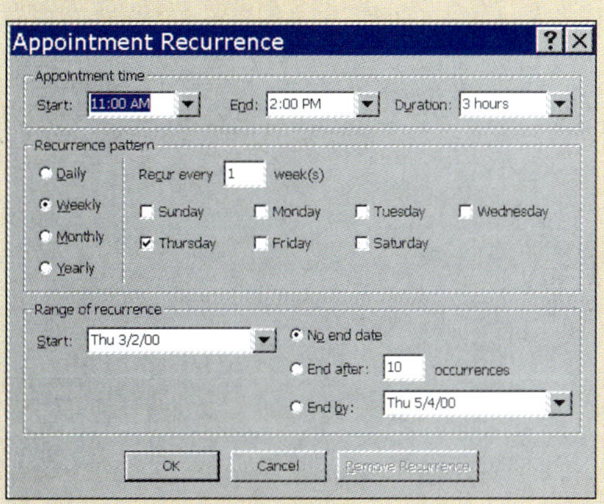

11 In the *Recurrence pattern* area:
SELECT: *Weekly* option button, if it isn't selected already

12 Review the other selections in the *Recurrence pattern* area. Also, note the selections in the *Range of recurrence* area. Use this area to specify when you want the appointment to start and end.

13 To leave the Appointment Recurrence dialog box and save the current appointment:
CLICK: OK command button
CLICK: Save and Close button on the Standard toolbar

14 Now, let's schedule an upcoming event. Let's pretend that in three weeks your school is sponsoring a Job Fair event that will take place on a Thursday and Friday.
CHOOSE: Actions, New All Day Event
The Event dialog box should appear. This dialog box is identical to the Appointment dialog box except that the *All day event* check box is selected.

15 Do the following to complete the *Subject* and *Location* text boxes:
TYPE: **Job Fair** in the *Subject* text box
CLICK: in the *Location* text box
TYPE: **School Stadium**

16 Using the *Start time* drop-down list, select the Thursday that is three weeks from this Thursday.

17 Using the *End time* drop-down list, select the Friday that is three weeks from this Friday.

18 To save the event for later reference:
CLICK: Save and Close button in the dialog box's toolbar
The two-day Job Fair event should be displaying in your calendar as a shaded bar spanning the two days.

19 Continue to the next lesson.

In Addition
Integrating Your Calendar with Other Outlook Tools

This box provides two examples of how your calendar data can be used in other parts of Outlook. First, when you display your calendar in Day or Week view, the TaskPad tool—which is integrated with the Tasks tool—appears for recording tasks related to the current day. (*Note:* We describe using the Tasks tool in the next module.) Second, you can easily send an appointment or event item as an e-mail attachment to others. To do this, open the calendar item and then choose Actions, Forward from the Menu bar. (*Note:* We describe sending e-mail in Chapter 3.)

2.1.3 Planning a Meeting

FEATURE
To take advantage of all that Outlook has to offer, big companies typically run a program called **Microsoft Exchange Server** on their networks. When Microsoft Exchange Server is used in conjunction with Outlook, users can collaborate and share information in ways that aren't possible using Outlook alone. For example, you can review your coworkers' calendars before coming up with a good meeting time, edit someone else's calendar directly, share contact information, and even give someone else the authority to answer your e-mail messages in the event you're unavailable.

METHOD

1. CLICK: Calendar icon ( ) in the Outlook Bar
2. CHOOSE: Actions, Plan a Meeting
3. Invite persons to attend your meeting.
4. View when your desired attendees are available.
5. Select a time when all attendees are available to meet.
6. CLICK: Make Meeting command button

PRACTICE

In this lesson, you review the steps required to plan a meeting using Outlook. You can perform the following steps even if Microsoft Exchange Server isn't running on your network.

Setup: Ensure that you've completed the previous lesson and that you're viewing your calendar using the Month view.

1 CHOOSE: Actions, Plan a Meeting
Your screen should now appear similar, but not identical, to Figure 2.7.

Figure 2.7
Plan a Meeting dialog box

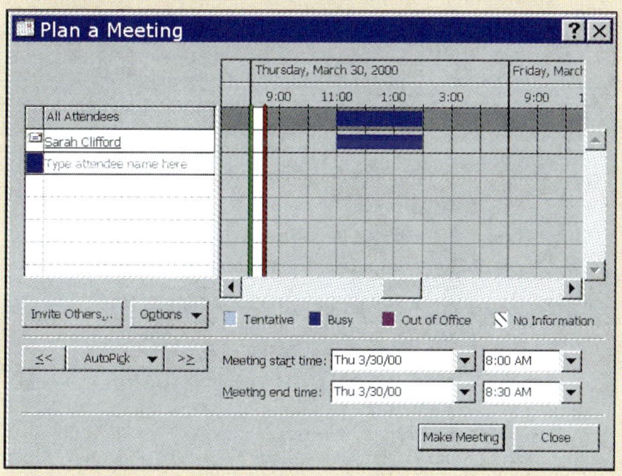

2 To select attendees for your meeting:
CLICK: Invite Others command button
Your screen should now appear similar, but not identical, to Figure 2.8. To make selections, click an attendee's name in the contact list box and then click the Required, Optional, or Resources command button. The attendee will be added to the *Message Recipients* list box. To remove an attendee, right-click the attendee's name in the *Message Recipients* list box and then choose Remove from the right-click menu.

Figure 2.8
Select Attendees and Resources dialog box

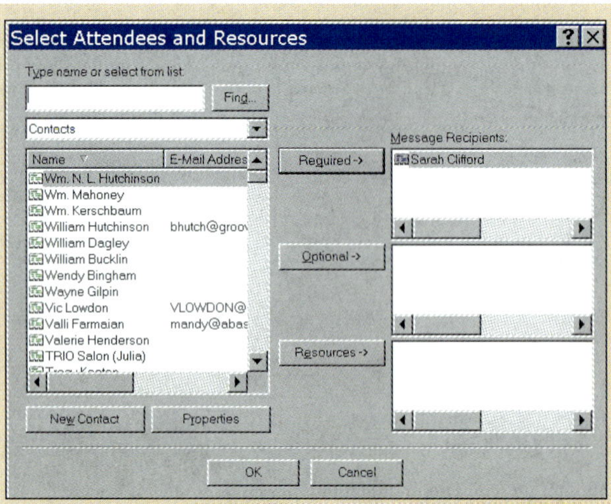

3. To leave this dialog box without adding an attendee:
CLICK: OK command button

4. Let's pretend you've added several people to your attendee list. Let's also assume that a good meeting time is one week from today at 1:00 PM. Locate that day and time using the horizontal scroll bar in the calendar grid.

5. CLICK: 1:00 PM on the day that is one week from today
A vertical bar showing a green border on the left (to represent the meeting's start time) and a red border on the right (to represent the meeting's end time) should appear in the 1:00 PM time slot. (*Note:* You can also use the *AutoPick* drop-down list to find the next time all attendees are available.)

6. To allot two hours for the meeting, drag the red border to the right until it is positioned in the 3:00 PM time slot. Figure 2.9 provides an example of the Plan a Meeting dialog box after allotting time for a two-hour meeting containing one attendee (you!).

Figure 2.9
Allotting two hours for a meeting

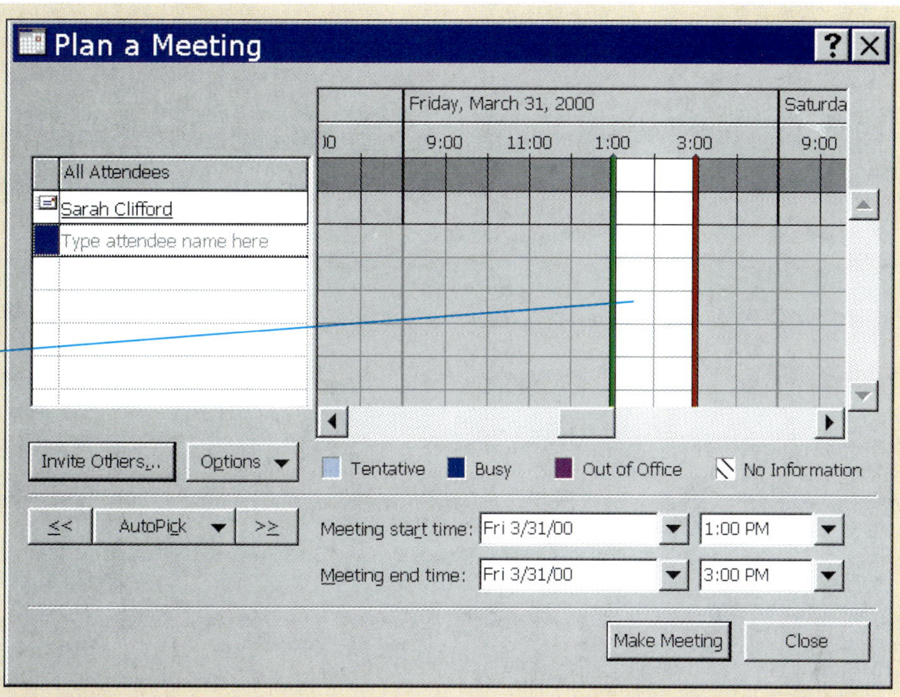

7 CLICK: Make Meeting command button
The Meeting window now appears (Figure 2.10) with the correct meeting time in the *Start time* and *End time* areas. If you had added attendees to your meeting, their e-mail addresses would automatically appear in the *To* text box. At this point, you would fill in the *Subject* and *Location* fields and include an optional note in the text area on the bottom of the window. As a final step you would click the Send button on the Standard toolbar to alert attendees of the upcoming meeting.

Figure 2.10
Meeting window

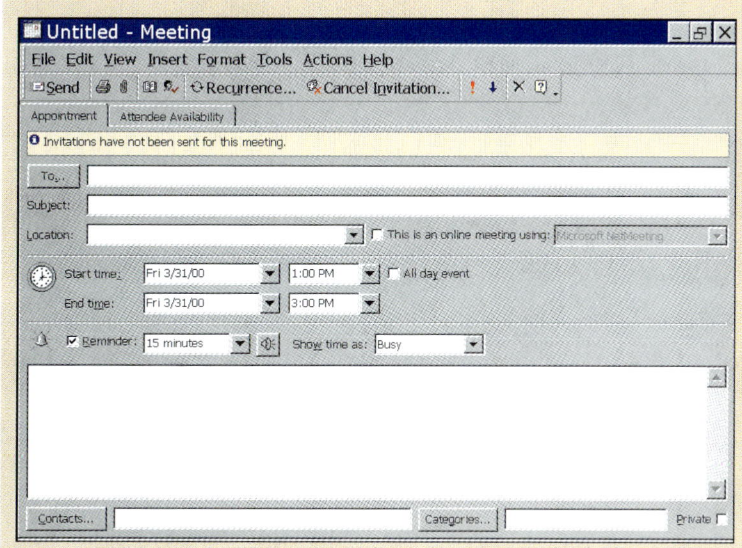

Recipients of your meeting request will receive your e-mail message with the following special buttons: Accept, Decline, Tentative, or Calendar. If the recipient clicks the Accept or Tentative buttons, the meeting will automatically be added to his or her calendar. If the recipient clicks the Decline button, you will be notified by e-mail that this recipient can't attend. If the recipient clicks the Calendar button, the recipient's calendar will display in a separate window so that he or she can check on availability.

8 To close the Meeting window without sending:
CLICK: Close button (☒) in the window's Title bar

9 To leave the Plan a Meeting dialog box:
CLICK: Close command button

In Addition
Booking Meeting Resources Directly

Not only can you schedule people to attend a meeting, you can also schedule resources, such as a meeting room, demonstration computer, slide projector, and so on. To schedule a resource, the resource must have its own e-mail address and Outlook calendar stored on the server computer. When you invite a resource to attend a meeting, the resource will automatically accept or reject the invitation based on its availability. To schedule a resource using the Calendar tool, choose Actions, Plan a Meeting and then click the Invite Others command button. Next, select the resource you want to schedule and then click the Resources command button. The resource will be added to the resources list on the right. After clicking the OK command button, proceed with selecting a meeting time and then sending out invitations.

2.1.4 Publishing Your Calendar

FEATURE

For those times when you want to refer to your calendar while away from your computer, you can print a copy of it. Outlook also makes it possible to convert your calendar for display on the World Wide Web. The process involves saving the calendar to **HTML** (Hypertext Markup Language) format for publishing to a Web server. Once the file is saved using the proper format, you may upload it to your company's Intranet or to a Web server.

METHOD

To print your calendar:

1. CHOOSE: File, Print
2. SELECT: a print style from the *Print style* list box
3. SELECT: a print range from the *Start* and *End* drop-down lists
4. Review the settings in the *Copies* area, making changes as necessary.
5. Optionally, customize your print settings by clicking the Page Setup command button and then clicking the OK command button when you're finished.
6. CLICK: OK command button to send your calendar to the printer

To save your calendar to HTML:

1. CHOOSE: File, Save as Web Page
2. SELECT: duration dates using the *Start date* and *End date* drop-down lists
3. Review the settings in the Options area, making changes as necessary.
4. Specify a Web page title and file name for your calendar in the *Save as* area.
5. CLICK: Save command button

PRACTICE

You will now print your calendar and save it as a Web page.

Setup: Ensure that you've completed the previous lesson and that you're viewing your calendar using the Month view.

1 To print your calendar:
CHOOSE: File, Print
The Print dialog box (Figure 2.11) should now appear.

Figure 2.11
Print dialog box

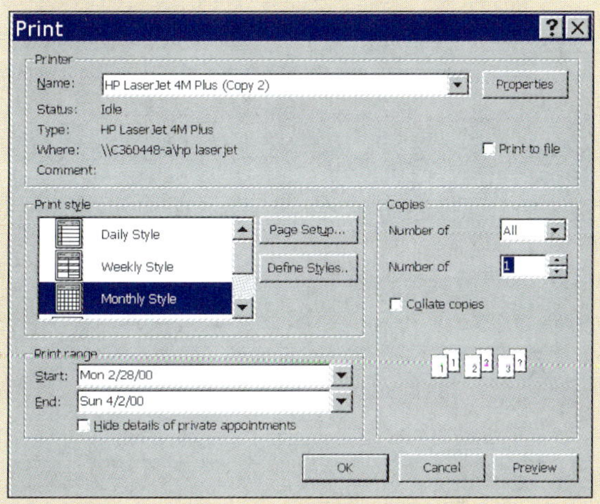

OUTLOOK

2. To see how your calendar will look printed in the Weekly Style:
SELECT: Weekly Style in the *Print style* list box
CLICK: Preview command button in the Print dialog box
Your screen should now appear similar, but not identical, to Figure 2.12.

Figure 2.12
Previewing the Weekly Style

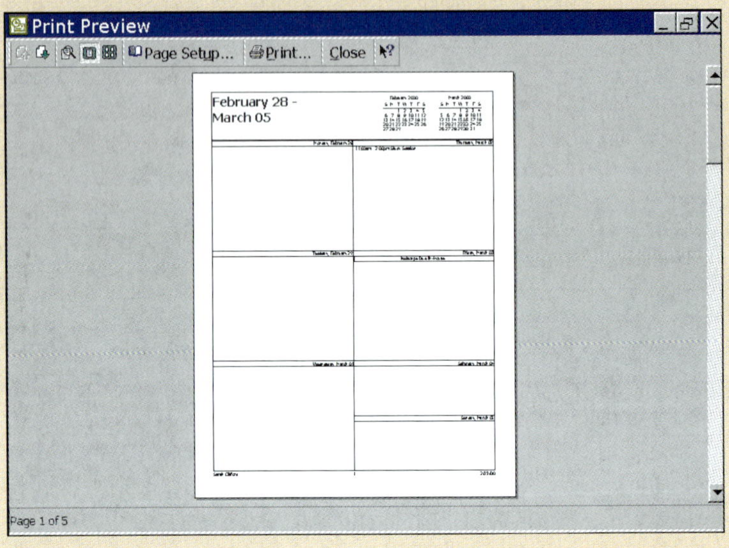

3. To return to the Print dialog box:
CLICK: Print button in the toolbar

4. To see how your calendar will look printed in the Monthly Style:
SELECT: Monthly Style in the *Print style* list box
CLICK: Preview command button
Your screen should now appear similar, but not identical, to Figure 2.13.

Figure 2.13
Previewing the Monthly Style

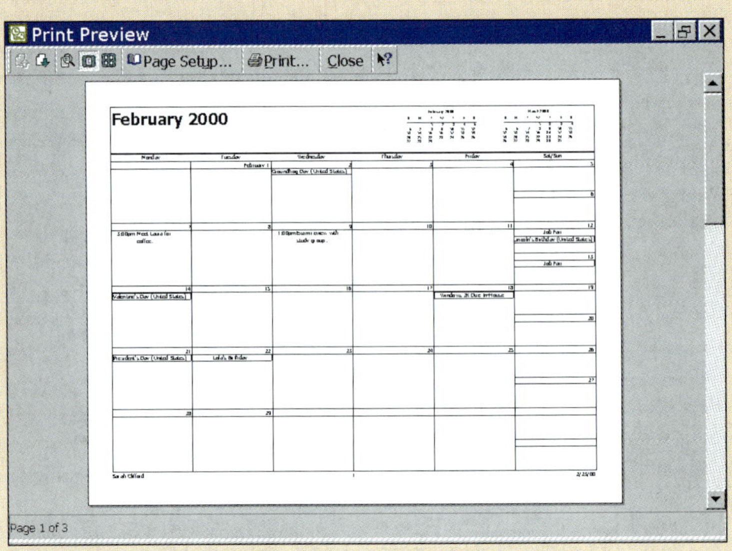

5 To return to the Print dialog box:
CLICK: Print button in the toolbar

6 To customize your print settings:
CLICK: Page Setup command button
The Page Setup dialog box should now appear (Figure 2.14). Using this dialog box you can change the layout of your calendar, displayed fonts, paper size, and header and footer information.

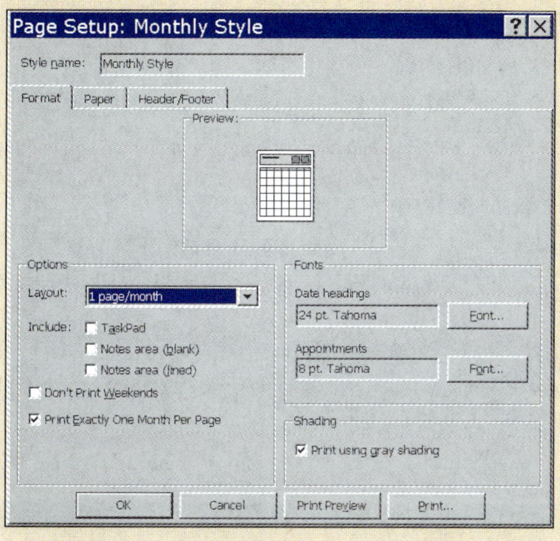

Figure 2.14
Page Setup dialog box

7 To leave this dialog box without making selections:
CLICK: Cancel command button

8 To print your calendar using the Monthly Style:
CLICK: OK command button
You now have a copy of your calendar for reference when you're away from your computer.

9 Now, let's save your calendar as a Web page.
CHOOSE: File, Save as Web Page
The Save as Web Page dialog box should now appear (Figure 2.15).

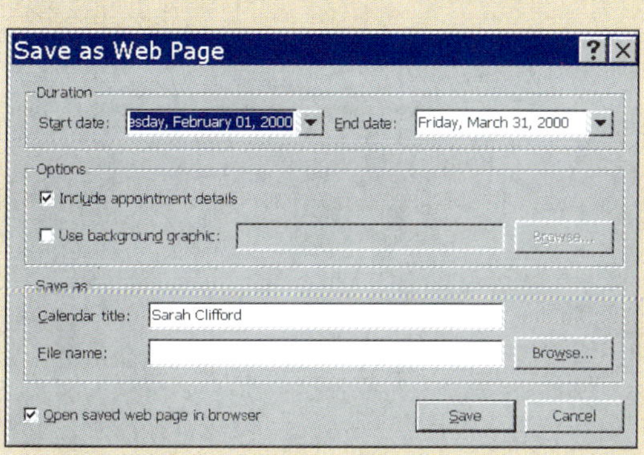

Figure 2.15
Save as Web Page dialog box

OUTLOOK

10 Review the different settings in this dialog box. Note the text that appears in the *Calendar title* text box. This text will appear at the top of your calendar on the Web page. You can edit this text as desired. Note also that the *Open saved web page in browser* check box is selected. As a result, your Web page will display in your browser upon your performing the save operation.

11 To save your Web page using the default selections:
CLICK: in the *File name* text box
TYPE: **My Calendar**

12 To select a save location:
CLICK: Browse command button
SELECT: a save location using the *Save in* drop-down list or Places bar
CLICK: Select command button
CLICK: Save command button
Your screen should now appear similar, but not identical, to Figure 2.16. (*Note:* To publish or post your Web calendar to an Intranet or to the Internet, click the Browse command button and then click the Web Folders button ( ) in the Places bar. As a last step, select a server location.)

Figure 2.16
Publishing your calendar to the Web

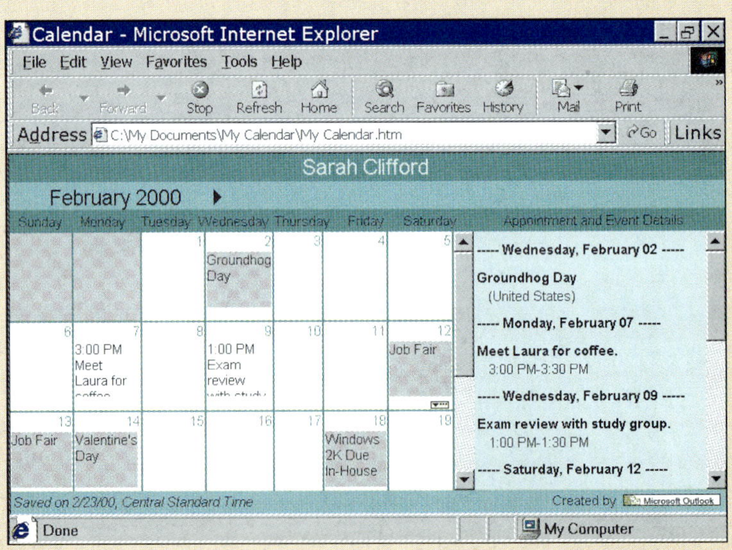

13 To close the Web browser window:
CLICK: its Close button ( )

14 Before finishing this module, we would like to lead you through deleting the appointment and event you added to your calendar in lesson 2.1.2.
CLICK: Job Fair event in your calendar
CLICK: Delete button (☒) on the Standard toolbar
CLICK: Study Session appointment in your calendar
CLICK: Delete button (☒) on the Standard toolbar
SELECT: *Delete all occurrences* option button
CLICK: OK command button

2.1 Self Check What is the procedure for saving your calendar to HTML for publishing on a Web server?

2.2 Managing Your Task List

The Tasks tool provides a convenient means for tracking tasks that you still need to perform or that are currently under way. You can use it to track just the names of your tasks or also include start and stop dates and assigned priorities. The Tasks tool might be considered Notes on overdrive. That is, whereas note items just sit there until you do something about them, task items can be programmed to remind you when a task should be completed with messages and alarms. You can also create tasks that must be completed on a recurring basis. In this module, you explore using the Tasks tool.

2.2.1 Creating Your Task List

FEATURE
When you initiate the command to add a task, Outlook displays two tabs for collecting information. These tabs contain preset forms that include many more blanks than you will probably ever use. You can simply enter the name of a task or go further and assign one or more details to the task. You can add tasks directly using the Tasks tool or using the TaskPad that appears in several Calendar views.

METHOD

1. CLICK: Tasks icon ( ) in the Outlook Bar
2. CLICK: New Task button ( ) on the Standard toolbar
3. CLICK: the tab you want to use and then fill in the relevant blanks
4. CLICK: Save and Close button on the Standard toolbar

PRACTICE

In this lesson, you add several tasks to your task list.

Setup: Ensure that Outlook is loaded.

1 Let's begin by accessing the Tasks tool.
CLICK: Tasks icon ( ) in the Outlook Bar

2 To add a task:
CLICK: New Task button ( ) on the Standard toolbar
The Task window should now appear.

3 Before continuing, ensure that the Task window is maximized. Your screen should now appear similar to Figure 2.17. To add a task, at a minimum you will complete the *Subject* text box. Optionally, you might specify a due date in the *Due date* area, assign a priority level to the task using the *Priority* drop-down list, and type an additional description in the text area.

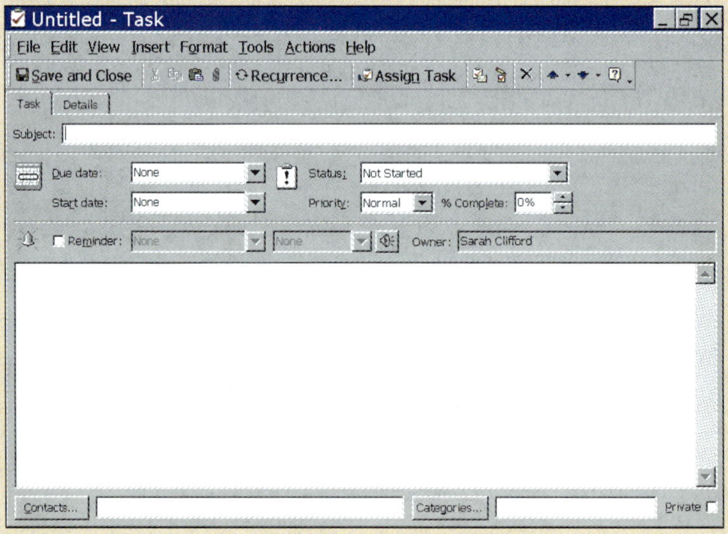

Figure 2.17
The Task Window: *Task* tab

4 The insertion point is blinking in the *Subject* text box.
TYPE: **Finalize the upcoming sales presentation.**

5 Since the date on your computer is different from ours, we aren't going to type in a due date or a start date. Let's look at what options are available in the *Status* drop-down list.
CLICK: *Status* drop-down arrow
Note that several options are displaying including In Progress, Completed, Waiting on someone else, and Deferred.

6 To leave the drop-down list without making a selection:
CLICK: *Status* drop-down arrow once more

7 To assign a High priority level to this task, do the following:
CLICK: *Priority* drop-down arrow
SELECT: High from the *Priority* drop-down list

8 Let's say that you've already completed approximately 75% of your sales presentation. To record this using the Tasks tool:
CLICK: up arrow in the *% Complete* spin box until 75% displays
Note that "In Progress" now appears in the *Status* drop-down list.

9 Let's take a peek at the *Details* tab.
CLICK: *Details* tab
The *Details* tab (Figure 2.18) is particularly useful for keeping track of business-related tasks. Let's leave this tab unchanged.

Figure 2.18

The Task Window: *Details* tab

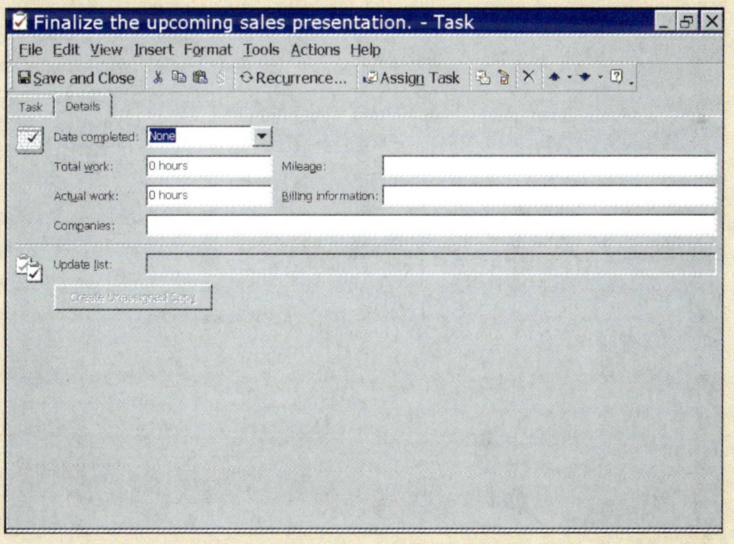

10 To save the current task:
CLICK: Save and Close button

OUTLOOK

11 Let's add a task to your task list using the TaskPad that is accessible using the Calendar tool.
CLICK: Calendar icon ( ) in the Outlook Bar
CLICK: Day button on the Standard toolbar
The TaskPad is displaying in the bottom-right corner of the Information Viewer. Note that the task you added previously appears in the task list.

12 In the TaskPad area:
CLICK: where it says "Click here to add a new Task"
TYPE: **Learn about Office 2000's integration features.**
PRESS: ENTER
The task item now appears in the TaskPad area.

13 CLICK: Tasks icon ( ) in the Outlook Bar
Note that the task you entered in step 12 appears in your task list.

14 Continue to the next lesson.

2.2.2 Viewing and Editing Your Task List

FEATURE

In Outlook, you can select to view your task list in different ways. You can select to view just those tasks that you're currently working on, those that are due in the next seven days, those that are already completed, and so on. You can also update existing tasks when their details change or when they have been completed.

METHOD

To view your task list:

CHOOSE: View, Current View, *option* from the Menu bar

To edit a task item:

1. DOUBLE-CLICK: the task item and then make your changes
2. CLICK: Save and Close button on the Standard toolbar

PRACTICE

This lesson leads you through displaying and editing your task list.

Setup: Ensure that you've completed the previous lesson and that your task list is displaying.

1 By default, your task list will display using the Simple List view. Let's change the current view:
CHOOSE: View, Current View, Detailed List
Your screen should now appear similar, but not identical, to Figure 2.19. Note that in this view additional information about your task appears. The exclamation mark next to the "Finalize the upcoming sales presentation" task indicates that this task is of high priority. Note also that the Status and % Complete columns display additional information about your tasks.

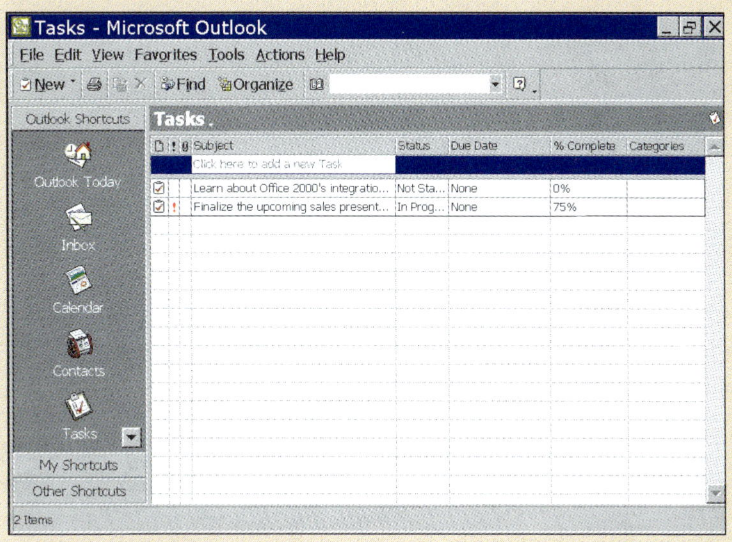

Figure 2.19
Listing tasks using the Detailed List view

2 Let's mark the "Finalize the upcoming sales presentation" task as completed.
DOUBLE-CLICK: "Finalize the upcoming sales presentation" task

3 CLICK: up arrow in the *% Complete* spin box until 100% displays
Note that "Completed" now appears in the *Status* drop-down list.

4 To save the updated task:
CLICK: Save and Close button on the Standard toolbar
Note that the task now appears crossed out in your task list.

5 To initiate the Print command:
CHOOSE: File, Print
Note that Table Style is selected in the *Print Style* list box.

6 To print your task using the default selections:
CLICK: OK command button

7 Continue to the next lesson.

OUTLOOK

2.2.3 Assigning Tasks to Others

FEATURE

When Microsoft Exchange Server is used in conjunction with Outlook, you can assign tasks to others and view their progress. Persons who have been assigned tasks will receive an e-mail message containing special buttons marked Accept and Decline. When a person clicks the Accept button, the task is automatically added to his or her task list. When a person clicks the Decline button, you're notified by e-mail that the person won't be able to perform the task. When declining tasks, it's usually a good idea to include an explanatory note.

METHOD

To assign a task to someone else:

1. RIGHT-CLICK: a task item
2. CHOOSE: Assign Task from the right-click menu
3. Fill in the recipient's e-mail address in the *To* text box.
4. CLICK: Send button on the Standard toolbar

To accept or decline a task:

1. CLICK: Accept button to add the task to your task list
2. CLICK: Decline button to respond to the sender that you're unable to perform the task

PRACTICE

In this lesson, you will begin the process of assigning a task to someone else. You can perform the following steps even if Microsoft Exchange Server isn't running on your network.

Setup: Ensure that you've completed the previous lessons in this module and that your task list is displaying.

1 To assign a task to someone else:
RIGHT-CLICK: "Learn about Office 2000's integration and Web features" task
CHOOSE: Assign Task from the right-click menu
Your screen should now appear similar to Figure 2.20.

Figure 2.20

Assigning a task to someone else

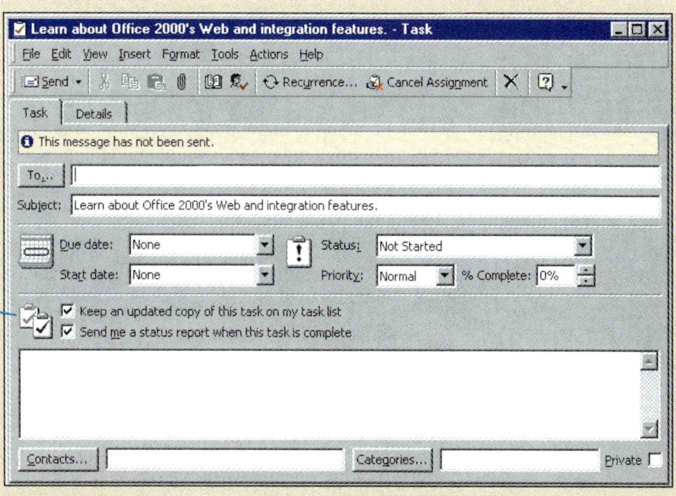

When these check boxes are selected, Outlook will maintain an updated copy of the task item on the task requester's computer and also inform the task requester when the task has been completed.

2 To send this task request to someone else, you would type their e-mail address in the *To* text box. Review the different details associated with this task.

3 Let's close the task window without saving.
CLICK: the window's Close button (☒)
CLICK: No command button

4 Figure 2.21 provides an example of a received task request. Note the Accept and Decline buttons. You simply click these buttons to register your response.

Figure 2.21

Receiving a task request

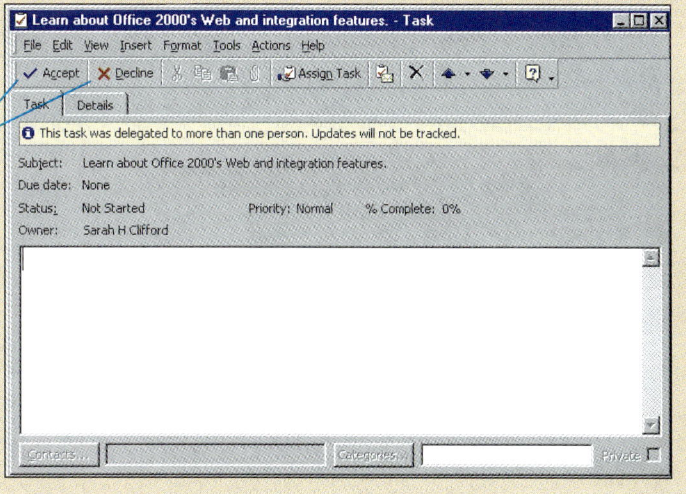

Accept and Decline buttons

OUTLOOK

2.2 Self Check What features of the Tasks tool do you find the most useful?

2.3 Getting Even More Organized

If you don't read another word in this learning guide, you will still be able to use Outlook effectively for managing contacts, appointments, and tasks. However, as the number of items in Outlook increases over time, you may find it difficult to quickly locate the information you need. Two methods for dealing with this problem involve assigning items to categories and creating folders. We describe both of these methods in this module.

2.3.1 Working with Categories

FEATURE
If you really want to get organized, you can assign Outlook items to categories. In Outlook, a *category* is a word or phrase that you can use for sorting, finding, and grouping items.

METHOD
To assign an item to a category:

1. RIGHT-CLICK: the item you want to assign
2. CHOOSE: Categories from the right-click menu
3. SELECT: one or more categories in the *Available categories* list box
4. CLICK: OK command button

To sort items based on their category:
CHOOSE: View, Current View, By Category

To find all items that have been assigned to the same category:
1. CHOOSE: Tools, Advanced Find
2. SELECT: "Any type of Outlook item" from the *Look for* drop-down list
3. CLICK: *More Choices* tab
4. CLICK: Categories command button
5. SELECT: a category in the *Available categories* list box
6. CLICK: OK command button
7. CLICK: Find Now command button

PRACTICE
In this lesson, you create a few Outlook items and assign them to categories. You will also find all items that have been assigned to the same category.

Setup: Ensure that Outlook is loaded.

1. On your own, use the Contacts tool to add the following contact item:

   Full Name: **Richard Hinge**
   Company: **Dolan's of Concord**
   Address: **2231 Monument Blvd**
   Concord, CA 94520
   Work phone: **925-686-1734**

2. On your own, use the Tasks tool to add the following task item:

   Order pre-hung entry door with side panels.

3. Let's assign the contact item you added in step 1 to the Suppliers category.
   CLICK: Contacts icon ( ) in the Outlook Bar
   RIGHT-CLICK: Richard Hinge's contact item
   CHOOSE: Categories
   The Categories dialog box will appear (Figure 2.22).

Figure 2.22
Categories dialog box

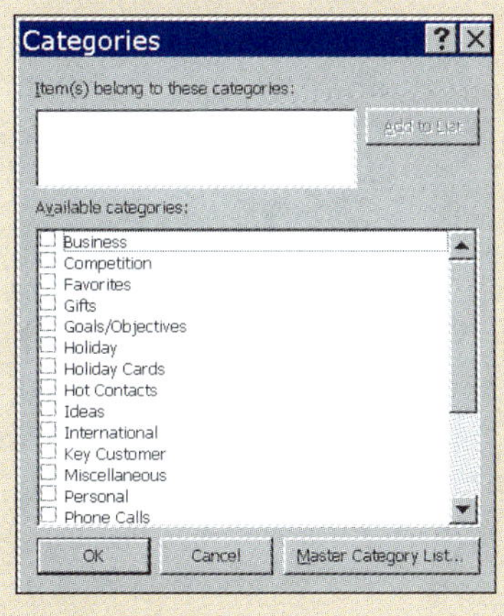

4. Locate the Suppliers category in the *Available categories* list box and then:
   SELECT: Suppliers category
   CLICK: OK command button

5. Let's assign the task item you added in step 2 to the Suppliers category.
   CLICK: Tasks icon ( ) in the Outlook Bar
   RIGHT-CLICK: "Order pre-hung entry door..." item
   CHOOSE: Categories
   SELECT: Suppliers category in the *Available categories* list box
   CLICK: OK command button

6 Let's sort your task list by category.
CHOOSE: View, Current View, By Category
Your screen should now appear similar to Figure 2.23. Categories are identified by gray bars in the Information Viewer. To display or hide items in a particular category, you must click the plus (+) or minus (−) sign located on the left side of the category bar.

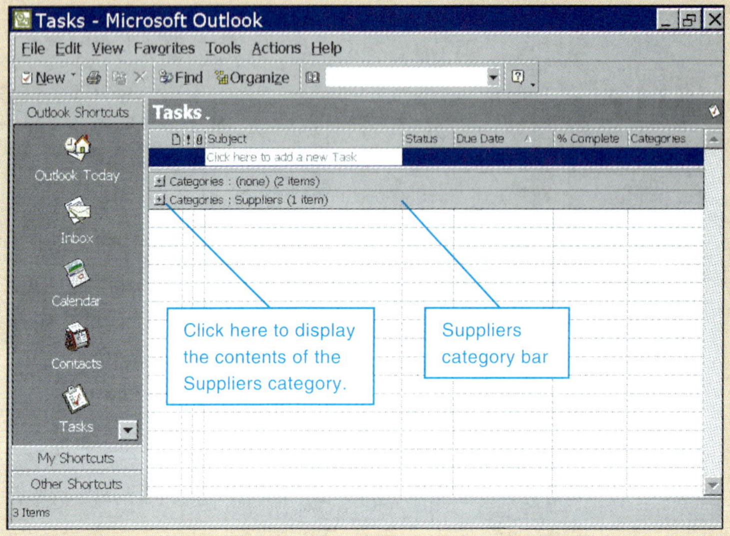

Figure 2.23
Sorting your task list by category

7 To display the contents of the Suppliers category
CLICK: plus sign (+) located on the left side of the "Categories: Suppliers" bar
The task item you created in step 2 should be displaying.

8 On your own, change the current view back to the Detailed List view.

9 You can also find all Outlook items, no matter what type, that have been assigned to the same category. This technique is useful for locating all items related to a particular project. To find all items assigned to the Suppliers category:
CHOOSE: Tools, Advanced Find
SELECT: "Any type of Outlook item" from the *Look for* drop-down list
CLICK: *More Choices* tab
CLICK: Categories command button
SELECT: Suppliers in the *Available categories* list box
CLICK: OK command button
CLICK: Find Now command button
The Advanced Find dialog box should now appear similar to Figure 2.24.

Figure 2.24

Finding all items that have been assigned to the same category

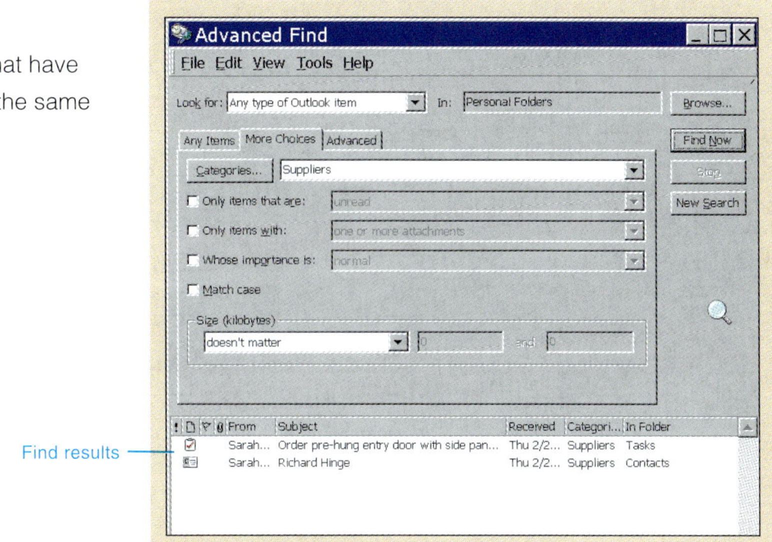

10 RIGHT-CLICK: Richard Hinge's contact item in the list area
Note that you can perform a number of procedures including opening, forwarding, and deleting the contact item.

11 To remove the right-click menu:
CLICK: Richard Hinge's contact item once more

12 You can also open items by double-clicking. To illustrate:
DOUBLE-CLICK: Richard Hinge's contact item in the list area

13 To close Richard Hinge's contact item:
CLICK: its Close button (☒)

14 To close the Advanced Find dialog box:
CLICK: its Close button (☒)

15 Continue to the next lesson.

2.3.2 Editing the Category List

FEATURE

You can choose from Outlook's preset list of categories such as Business, Personal, Hot Contacts, and Key Customer, or you can add new categories and assign items to them. You can also delete categories that you won't ever use.

METHOD

1. CHOOSE: Edit, Categories from the Menu bar
2. CLICK: Master Category List command button
3. Use the Add, Delete, and Reset command buttons to modify the categories list.
4. CLICK: OK command button twice

PRACTICE

You will now practice modifying the master category list.

Setup: Ensure that you've completed the previous lesson and that your task list is displaying.

1 Let's add a new category to the master category list. Before editing the master category list, you must select an Outlook item.
CLICK: any item in your task list
CHOOSE: Edit, Categories
CLICK: Master Category List command button
The Master Category List dialog box should now appear (Figure 2.25). The insertion point is blinking in the *New* text box.

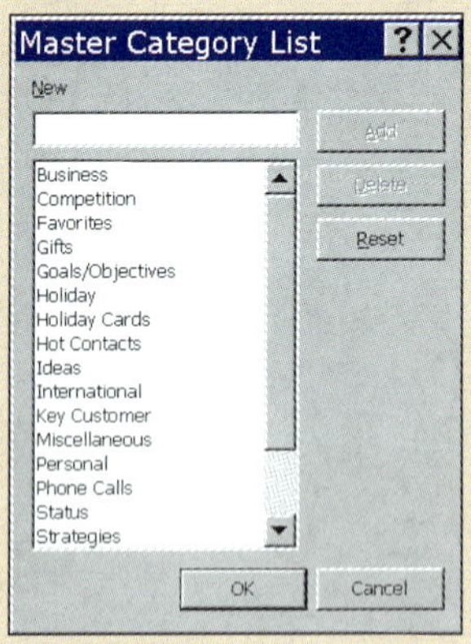

Figure 2.25
Master Category List dialog box

2. To add a category named Friends:
TYPE: **Friends** in the *New* text box
CLICK: Add command button
CLICK: OK command button
Note that the Friends category now appears in the *Available categories* list box.

3. Let's delete a category.
CLICK: Master Category List command button
CLICK: Competition category in the list box
CLICK: Delete command button
The Competition category was removed from the category list.

4. To reset the category list to what it was originally:
CLICK: Reset command button
CLICK: OK command button to reset the list

5. To proceed:
CLICK: OK to leave the Master Category List dialog box
CLICK: OK to leave the Categories dialog box

6. Continue to the next lesson.

2.3.3 Working with Folders

FEATURE

In Outlook, items are stored in *folders*, with each folder containing the same type of item. By default, contact items are stored in the Contacts folder, appointment items are stored in the Calendar folder, task items are stored in the Tasks folder, and so on. As these folders fill up, you will want to use techniques for locating items easily. You can either use categories, as described in the last two lessons, or create new folders altogether.

METHOD

To create a new folder:

1. CHOOSE: File, New, Folder from the Menu bar
2. TYPE: a name for the new folder in the *Name* text box
3. CHOOSE: the type of item you want to store in the folder from the *Folder contains* drop-down list
4. CLICK: in the hierarchical list of folders where you want to store the new folder
5. CLICK: OK command button

To move items between folders:

1. Locate the item you want to move in the Information Viewer.
2. DRAG: the item to the desired folder icon in the Outlook Bar

PRACTICE

In this lesson, you create a new folder for storing business contacts. You will then move an existing contact into the new folder.

Setup: Ensure that you've completed the previous lessons in this module and that your task list is displaying.

1 Let's create a new folder called "Business Contacts." Do the following:
CHOOSE: File, New, Folder
The Create New Folder dialog box should now appear (Figure 2.26).

Figure 2.26
Create New Folder dialog box

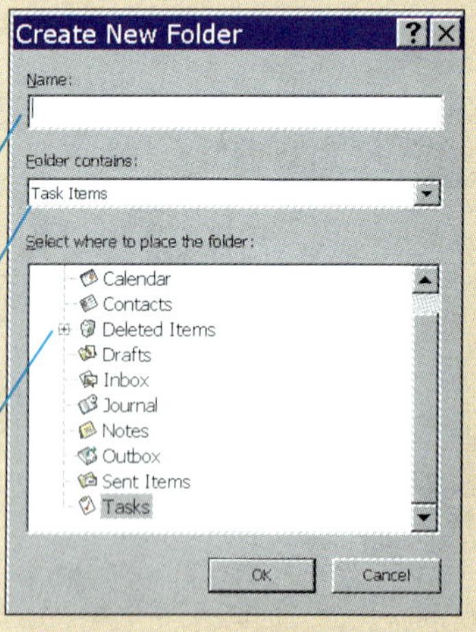

2 In the *Name* text box:
TYPE: **Business Contacts**

3 In the *Folder contains* drop-down list:
SELECT: Contact Items

4 In the *Select where to place the folder* hierarchical diagram:
CLICK: Contacts

5 To create the folder:
CLICK: OK command button

6 If the following dialog box appears asking you whether you want a shortcut added to the Outlook bar, click the Yes command button. The new folder shortcut was added to the My Shortcuts group.

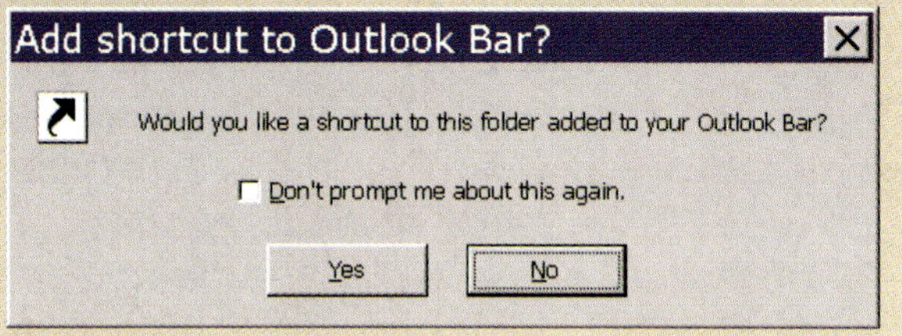

7 To view the contents of the new folder:
CLICK: My Shortcuts group button in the Outlook Bar
CLICK: Business Contacts icon ( )
As you can see, no items are currently stored in the Business Contacts folder.

8 Let's move Richard Hinge's contact information from the Contacts folder into the Business Contacts folder.
CLICK: Outlook Shortcuts group button in the Outlook Bar
CLICK: Contacts icon ( ) in the Outlook Bar

9 Locate Richard Hinge's contact item in the Information Viewer area and then:
DRAG: Richard Hinge's contact item into the Business Contacts folder located in the My Shortcuts group

10 Since we created the "Business Contacts" folder for instructional purposes only, as a final step let's delete the Business Contacts folder. First, let's remove the Business Contacts icon from the Outlook Bar.
CLICK: My Shortcuts group button
RIGHT-CLICK: Business Contacts icon
CHOOSE: "Remove from Outlook Bar" from the right-click menu
CLICK: Yes command button to remove the shortcut

11 To remove the Business Contacts folder:
CHOOSE: View, Folder List
RIGHT-CLICK: Business Contacts folder in the folder list
CHOOSE: Delete "Business Contacts" from the right-click menu
CLICK: Yes command button

OUTLOOK

12 To hide the folder list
CHOOSE: View, Folder List

2.3.4 Using the Office Clipboard

FEATURE

In Microsoft Office 2000 applications, the Windows and Office Clipboards enable you to copy items from one location to another. Whereas the **Windows Clipboard** can store only a single item at once, the enhanced **Office Clipboard** can store up to 12 items. The Office Clipboard is ideal for assembling reports that require excerpts from multiple documents or Outlook items. The Office Clipboard is automatically activated when you copy two items without an intervening paste. Whereas the contents of the Windows Clipboard are pasted by clicking the Paste button () on the Standard toolbar, the contents of the Office Clipboard are pasted using buttons on the Clipboard toolbar. Using the Clipboard toolbar, you can paste the items into any one of the Office 2000 applications individually or as a group. You can also clear the entire contents of the Office Clipboard with a button on the Clipboard toolbar.

METHOD

To copy an item to the Office Clipboard:

1. Open an item in Outlook.
2. CLICK: Copy button () on the Standard toolbar

To paste items from the Office Clipboard:

- CLICK: an item's icon on the Clipboard toolbar to paste an individual item
- CLICK: Paste All button (Paste All) on the Clipboard toolbar to paste all items at once

PRACTICE

In this lesson, you copy two tasks to the Office Clipboard and then paste them into a new task item.

Setup: Ensure that you've completed the previous lessons in this module.

1. Let's open an existing task and then copy its description to the Office Clipboard.
   DOUBLE-CLICK: "Order pre-hung entry door..." item in your Tasks list
   The task should be displaying in a separate task window.

2. Let's copy the text in the *Subject* text box to the Office Clipboard:
   CLICK: three times in the *Subject* text box to select its contents
   CLICK: Copy button ( ) on the Standard toolbar

3. To close the current task window:
   CLICK: its Close button ( )

4. On your own, open another task and then copy the text in the *Subject* text box to the Office Clipboard. After completing this step, the Office Clipboard should display two icons representing the two copied tasks, as shown below.

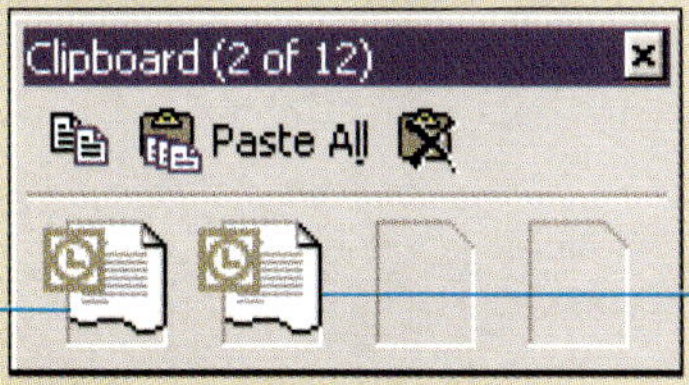

5. Close the current task window by clicking its Close button ( ).

6. To illustrate the capabilities of the Office Clipboard, let's paste its contents into a new task window. To begin:
   CLICK: New Task button ( ) on the Standard toolbar
   TYPE: **Complete all tasks** in the *Subject* text box
   CLICK: in the large text area in the bottom of the window
   CLICK: the icon on the Clipboard toolbar representing the first item you copied
   PRESS: ENTER
   CLICK: the icon on the Clipboard toolbar representing the second item you copied
   (*Note:* You could also have clicked the Paste All button (Paste All), but the task items wouldn't have displayed on separate lines.)

7. To save the current task:
   CLICK: Save and Close button

8. To clear the contents of the Office Clipboard:
   CLICK: Clear Clipboard button ( ) on the Clipboard toolbar

9. To close the Office Clipboard:
   CLICK: its Close button ( )

2.3 Self Check In Outlook, what are categories used for?

2.4 Customizing Your Workspace

On installing Microsoft Outlook, you'll find the Menu bar and toolbars set up in a default configuration. As you gain experience with Outlook, you may want to customize it to your preferred way of working. Fortunately, Outlook's environment is extremely flexible and easily customized. For example, you can modify the existing interface elements, such as the Menu bar, and create entirely new menu options and toolbars. Whatever your efforts involve, your overall objective should be to make it easier to access the commands and procedures you use most often.

2.4.1 Manipulating Toolbars

FEATURE

Toolbars allow you to organize multiple commands and features into compact and conveniently located button strips. The Standard toolbar itself gives you single-click access to several commands. In addition to its built-in toolbars, Outlook allows you to create custom toolbars that are suited to your personal needs and preferences. Do you know that Outlook's menu is actually a toolbar? Like all toolbars, you can display the Menu bar docked alongside the application window or *floating* in its own window, complete with a Title bar and Close button ( ). There are four docking areas for toolbars, alongside the top and bottom horizontal window borders and the left and right window borders.

METHOD

- To float a toolbar, drag it away from the four docking areas using the move handle that appears at the far left-hand side of a docked toolbar.
- To dock a toolbar, drag it by its Title bar to the top, bottom, left, or right wall in the application window.
- To display or hide a toolbar, choose View, Toolbars or right-click on a displayed toolbar and then choose the toolbar's name.

PRACTICE

In this lesson, you practice manipulating the display and appearance of toolbars.

Setup: Ensure that Outlook is loaded.

1. To ensure that your screen looks the same as ours:
CLICK: Contacts icon ( ) in the Outlook Bar

2. A narrow vertical bar, called a *move handle*, is located on the left side of every toolbar. Do the following to move the Standard toolbar:
DRAG: the move handle of the Standard toolbar toward the center of the application window

3. When you release the mouse button, the Standard toolbar appears in its own window.

4. To size the toolbar, position the mouse on the Standard toolbar's right-hand border until the pointer changes to a horizontal double-headed arrow. Then, drag the toolbar's border inward until the toolbar contains three rows, as shown below, and release the mouse button.

5. On your own, drag the Standard toolbar by its Title bar back to its original position below the Menu bar.

6. To view the most commonly used toolbars in Outlook:
CHOOSE: View, Toolbars
You should see a minimum of 3 toolbars listed in the cascading menu. The toolbars that are active and displayed in the application window are shown with a check mark (✔) in the menu.

7. Let's activate a new toolbar:
CHOOSE: Web
The Web toolbar should now appear at the same location where it was last activated.

8. To close the Web toolbar using the right-click menu:
RIGHT-CLICK: an existing toolbar
CHOOSE: Web to deselect it

9. Continue to the next lesson.

2.4.2 Customizing Toolbars

FEATURE

Besides having the ability to control where toolbars are positioned in the application window, you can modify the location of buttons in a toolbar, size buttons, add and delete buttons, and even create new buttons that are assigned to run macros. Moving buttons on a toolbar offers limited scope for personalizing your system. However, removing buttons that you don't often use and replacing them with frequently used commands and features can improve your productivity tenfold.

METHOD

To add, delete, and modify toolbar buttons:

1. CHOOSE: Tools, Customize
2. DRAG: buttons and commands within a toolbar to change the order; away from a toolbar to delete it; or onto a toolbar to add it
3. RIGHT-CLICK: a toolbar button to display editing commands
4. CLICK: Close command button when finished

To reset a toolbar to its default configuration:

1. CHOOSE: Tools, Customize
2. CLICK: *Toolbars* tab
3. SELECT: the desired toolbar in the Toolbars list box
4. CLICK: Reset command button
5. CLICK: OK command button to confirm

PRACTICE

In this lesson, you modify the contents of a toolbar. The procedures described in this lesson can also be used to modify the Menu bar.

Setup: Ensure that you've completed the previous lesson in this module and that your contacts list is displaying in the Information Viewer.

1. To customize a toolbar, you access the Customize dialog box. Do the following:
CHOOSE: Tools, Customize
CLICK: *Toolbars* tab
The dialog box shown in Figure 2.27 appears.

Figure 2.27
Customize dialog box: *Toolbars* tab

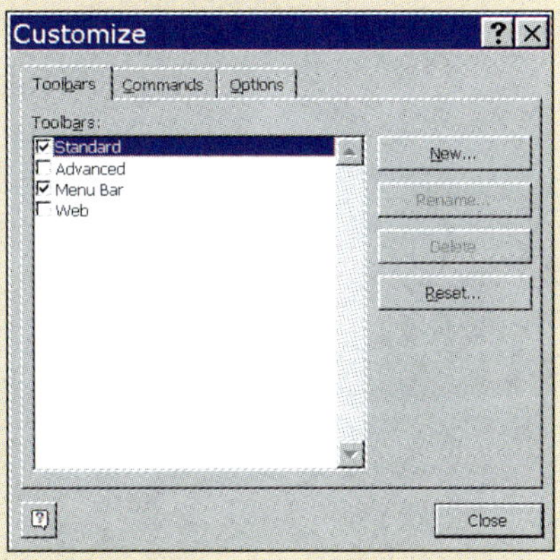

2. When the Customize dialog box is displayed, all of the toolbar buttons and menu commands are disabled. Therefore, you can move and remove buttons on a toolbar by simply clicking and dragging them. To illustrate, do the following:
CLICK: Organize button (Organize) on the Standard toolbar
The button appears surrounded by a thick border.

3. To remove this button from the toolbar:
DRAG: Organize button (Organize) away from the toolbar and into the Information Viewer

4. Release the mouse button to complete the button removal. (*Note:* You can also change the order of buttons on a toolbar or Menu bar by dragging them to their new locations.)

5. To size the drop-down list button on the Standard toolbar:
CLICK: *Find a Contact* drop-down arrow ( )

6. Position the mouse pointer over the right vertical border of the button until the mouse pointer changes shape. Then, drag the border to the right to increase its width. Release the mouse button to view the results.

7. To add a button for creating a new note item:
CLICK: *Commands* tab in the Customize dialog box
The Customize dialog box should now appear similar to Figure 2.28.

Figure 2.28
Customize dialog box: *Commands* tab

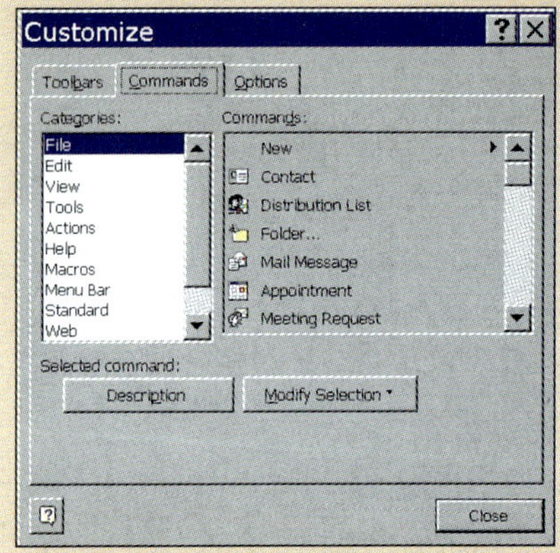

8. SELECT: File in the *Categories* list box
SELECT: Note in the *Commands* list box

9. Drag the Note option from the *Commands* list box and position it, using the black insertion line as your guide, to the right of the Find button.

10. Release the mouse button. You will see that the Note button appears in the toolbar.

11. Fortunately, Outlook provides a command that lets you reset the toolbars back to their original settings. To do so:
CLICK: *Toolbars* tab

12. To reset the Standard toolbar, ensure that it is highlighted in the list box and then:
CLICK: Reset command button
CLICK: OK command button to reset any changes made to the Standard toolbar

13. To close the Customize dialog box and accept the changes:
CLICK: Close command button

2.4 Self Check What procedure would you use to remove a button from the Standard toolbar?

2.5 Chapter Review

Two tools that can really help you take care of business are Outlook's Calendar and Tasks tools. Not only do these tools work well by themselves, but they also work well together. That is, any tasks that you enter using Calendar's TaskPad are automatically recorded in your task list. As you add more and more items to Outlook over time, you'll want to know how to deal with them. Two useful methods for dealing with lots of Outlook items involve assigning them to categories and creating folders. To further boost your productivity, you can customize Outlook's Menu bar and toolbars to your preferred way of working.

2.5.1 Command Summary

Many of the commands and procedures appearing in this chapter are summarized in the following table.

Skill Set	To Perform This Task . . .	Do the Following . . .
Using the Outlook 2000 Calendar	View your calendar	• CLICK: Go to Today button, Day button, Week button, or Month button on the Standard toolbar • CHOOSE: View, Current View, *option* from the Menu bar
	Customize your calendar	CHOOSE: Tools, Options CLICK: Calendar Options command button
	Schedule an appointment	CLICK: Calendar icon ( ) in the Outlook Bar CLICK: New Appointment button ( )
	Schedule an event	CLICK: Calendar icon ( ) in the Outlook Bar CHOOSE: Actions, New All Day Event

Continued

Skill Set	To Perform This Task . . .	Do the Following . . .
Using the Outlook 2000 Calendar *Continued*	Plan a meeting	CLICK: Calendar icon ( ) in the Outlook Bar CLICK: New Appointment button ( )
	Schedule an appointment	CLICK: Calendar icon ( ) in the Outlook Bar CLICK: New Appointment button ( )
	Schedule an event	CLICK: Calendar icon ( ) in the Outlook Bar CHOOSE: Actions, New All Day Event
	Plan a meeting	CLICK: Calendar icon ( ) in the Outlook Bar CHOOSE: Actions, Plan a Meeting
	Print your calendar	CHOOSE: File, Print
	Save your calendar to HTML	CHOOSE: File, Save as Web Page
Using Tasks	Add a task	CLICK: Tasks icon ( ) in the Outlook Bar CLICK: New Task button ( )
	View your task list	CHOOSE: View, Current View, *option*
	Edit a task item	DOUBLE-CLICK: a task item
	Assign a task to someone else	RIGHT-CLICK: a task item CHOOSE: Assign Task
	Accept or decline a task	1. Open a received task item. 2. CLICK: Accept or Decline button on the Standard toolbar

Continued

Skill Set	To Perform This Task . . .	Do the Following . . .
Navigating and Using Outlook 2000 Effectively	Assign an item to a category	RIGHT-CLICK: the item you want to assign CHOOSE: Categories
	Sort items based on their category	CHOOSE: View, Current View, By Category
	Find all items assigned to the same category	CHOOSE: Tools, Advanced Find SELECT: "Any type of Outlook item" from the *Look for* drop-down list CLICK: *More Choices* tab CLICK: Categories command button SELECT: a category CLICK: OK command button CLICK: Find Now command button
	Edit the master category list	CHOOSE: Edit, Categories
	Create a folder	CHOOSE: File, New, Folder
	Move items between folders	DRAG: the item to the desired folder
	Paste the contents of the Office Clipboard as a group	CLICK: Paste All button (Paste All) on the Clipboard toolbar
	Clear the contents of the Office Clipboard	CLICK: Clear Clipboard button ( ) on the Clipboard toolbar
Working with Toolbars	Customize the Menu bar and toolbars	CHOOSE: Tools, Customize CLICK: *Commands* tab for Menu bar, or *Toolbars* tab
	Toggle the display of a toolbar on and off	CHOOSE: View, Toolbars CHOOSE: *the desired toolbar*

2.5.2 Key Terms

This section specifies page references for the key terms identified in this chapter. For a complete list of definitions, refer to the Glossary provided immediately after the Appendix in this learning guide.

HTML, *p. 64*

Microsoft Exchange Server, *p. 60*

Office Clipboard, *p. 84*

Windows Clipboard, *p. 84*

2.6 Review Questions

2.6.1 Short Answer

1. In Outlook, what is the difference between an appointment and an event?
2. What additional capabilities become available when Microsoft Exchange Server is used in conjunction with Outlook?
3. Using the Tasks folder, how would you go about crossing a task off your list?
4. In Outlook, what is a category?
5. How is the Office Clipboard different from the Windows Clipboard?
6. What is the procedure for deleting an Outlook item?
7. What is needed before you can assign tasks to others?
8. What dialog box must you use to customize most of Outlook's tools?
9. In what ways can you customize your Outlook calendar?
10. In Outlook, why might you want to create a new folder?

2.6.2 True/False

1. ____ The Calendar tool can be used to add tasks to your task list.
2. ____ An Outlook task item can be programmed to remind you when a task should be completed.
3. ____ The Outlook Bar can contain a maximum of ten folders.
4. ____ Calendar provides the most convenient tool for managing appointments.
5. ____ It's possible to publish your Outlook calendar on the Web.
6. ____ In Outlook, items are stored in folders, with each folder containing the same type of item.
7. ____ The Menu bar can't be moved from its docked position below the Title bar.

8. ____ In Outlook, it's possible to add, delete, and modify toolbar buttons.
9. ____ It's possible to import your country's holidays into your calendar.
10. ____ In Outlook, an appointment doesn't have a start and end time.

2.6.3 Multiple Choice

1. An Outlook folder can store:
   a. names and addresses
   b. e-mail messages
   c. interview appointments
   d. all of the above

2. Which of the following command sequences enables you to add a folder to the Outlook bar?
   a. Insert, Folder
   b. File, New, Folder
   c. Insert, Outlook Folder
   d. all of the above

3. In Outlook, it's possible to:
   a. assign tasks to others
   b. invite others to meetings
   c. decline a task assignment
   d. all of the above

4. Which of the following makes it possible to collaborate and share information with others?
   a. Microsoft Outlook
   b. Microsoft Exchange Server
   c. a and b, when used together
   d. None of the above

5. Which of the following is used for sorting, finding, and grouping Outlook items?
   a. Microsoft Exchange Server
   b. categories
   c. Office Clipboard
   d. Advanced Find dialog box

6. Which of the following lets you list all Outlook items, no matter what type, that have been assigned to the same category?
   a. Microsoft Exchange Server
   b. categories
   c. Office Clipboard
   d. Advanced Find dialog box

7. It's possible to make the following changes to Outlook's master category list:
   a. add categories
   b. delete categories
   c. reset the category list
   d. all of the above

8. In Outlook, you move items between folders by:
   a. dragging
   b. clicking
   c. double-clicking
   d. all of the above

9. In Office applications, which of the following enables you to copy items from one location to another?
   a. Windows Clipboard
   b. Office Clipboard
   c. both a and b
   d. Menu bar

10. Which of the following tasks can you perform with the Clipboard toolbar?
   a. paste individual items
   b. paste items as a group
   c. clear the contents of the Office Clipboard
   d. all of the above

2.7 Hands-On Projects

2.7.1 Creative Design Picture Framing: Scheduling an Appointment

In this exercise, you practice using the Calendar tool to schedule and edit an appointment, display different calendar views, and print a calendar page.

1. Let's use the Calendar tool to schedule an appointment with a client who is eager to frame a valuable painting. To ensure you are viewing this month's calendar:
   CLICK: Calendar icon ( ) in the Outlook Bar
   CLICK: Go to Today button on the Standard toolbar to ensure that today's date is displayed
   CLICK: Month button ( ) on the Standard toolbar to view this month at a glance

2. To open the Appointment window:
   CLICK: New Appointment button (icon) on the Standard toolbar
3. To add text to the Subject text box:
   TYPE: **Mrs. Bradley's original Picasso painting**
4. To schedule the date of Mrs. Bradley's framing appointment:
   CLICK: down arrow to the right of the date in the *Start time* area
   CHOOSE: *the next Tuesday from today*
5. To schedule the time of Mrs. Bradley's appointment:
   CLICK: down arrow to the right of the time in the *Start time* area
   CHOOSE: 9:00 AM from the drop-down list
6. Since Mrs. Bradley must leave your appointment for an antique auction that begins at 11:00:
   CLICK: down arrow next to the time in the *End time* area
   CHOOSE: 10:30 AM from the drop-down list
7. To remind yourself one hour prior to the commencement of this important meeting:
   SELECT: the *Reminder* check box, if not already selected
   CLICK: down arrow next to the time in the *Reminder* area
   CHOOSE: 1 hour from the *Reminder* drop-down list
8. To save Mrs. Bradley's appointment:
   CLICK: Save and Close button on the Standard toolbar
9. To display Mrs. Bradley's appointment using a different calendar view:
   CLICK: *on Mrs. Bradley's appointment date* to select it
   CLICK: Day button (icon) on the Standard toolbar
10. To view Mrs. Bradley's appointment in Week view:
    CLICK: Week button on the Standard toolbar
11. Mrs. Bradley just phoned to inform you that the antique auction has been canceled and she is now able to discuss her framing requirements with you until 11:00 AM. To edit Mrs. Bradley's appointment window:
    DOUBLE-CLICK: Mrs. Bradley's appointment item in your calendar
12. To change the end time of Mrs. Bradley's appointment:
    CLICK: down arrow next to the time in the *End time* area
    CHOOSE: 11:00 AM from the drop-down list
    CLICK: Save and Close button on the Standard toolbar
13. To print a copy of your calendar displaying the day of Mrs. Bradley's appointment:
    CHOOSE: File, Print
    SELECT: Daily Style from the *Print style* area
    SELECT: the date of Mrs. Bradley's appointment from the *Start* drop-down list in the *Print range* area
    SELECT: the date of Mrs. Bradley's appointment from the *End* drop-down list in the *Print range* area
14. To preview how the printed copy will look:
    CLICK: Preview command button in the Print dialog box

15. To print the previewed page:
    CLICK: Print command button in the Print Preview toolbar
    CLICK: OK command button in the Print dialog box

2.7.2 Summit Career College: Recording a Task

You will now practice using the Tasks tool to schedule, view, and print a new task.

1. To access the Tasks tool and add a new task:
   CLICK: Tasks icon ( ) in the Outlook Bar
   CLICK: New Task button ( ) on the Standard toolbar
2. To add text to the *Subject* text box:
   TYPE: **Career Fair Planning**
3. Since the Career Fair will be held on a Friday in three weeks from today, do the following:
   CLICK: down arrow to the right of the date in the *Due date* area
   CHOOSE: the next Friday three weeks from today
4. To record that you started preparing for the Career Fair last Friday, do the following:
   CLICK: down arrow to the right of the date in the *Start date* area
   CHOOSE: the past Friday from today
   CLICK: *Status* drop-down arrow
   SELECT: In Progress from the *Status* drop-down list
5. To assign a high priority level to this task:
   CLICK: *Priority* drop-down arrow
   SELECT: High from the *Priority* drop-down list
6. To record that 25% of this task has already been completed:
   CLICK: down arrow in the *% Complete* spin box until 25% displays
7. To complete several final details prior to the Career Fair, let's specify that a reminder displays one day before the big event:
   SELECT: the *Reminder* check box, if not already selected
   CLICK: down arrow next to the date in the *Reminder* area
   CHOOSE: *the Thursday prior to the Career Fair*
   CLICK: down arrow next to the time in the *Reminder* area
   CHOOSE: 9:00 AM from the drop-down list
8. To save this Career Fair planning task:
   CLICK: Save and Close button
9. To view your task on a timeline:
   CHOOSE: View, Current View, Task Timeline and then use the horizontal scroll bar to view the start and end dates for the task
10. Now let's view a list of your active tasks:
    CHOOSE: View, Current View, Active Tasks

11. To print a copy of this task:
    CHOOSE: File, Print
    SELECT: Memo Style in the *Print Style* list box
    CLICK: OK command button
12. After successfully printing it, delete the Career Fair Planning task:
    SELECT: Career Fair Planning task item in your task list
    CLICK: Delete button (☒) on Standard toolbar

2.7.3 Rapunzel's Hair Design: Creating a Recurring Appointment and Customizing Your Calendar

In this exercise schedule a recurring event, customize your calendar, and print your calendar in the Monthly view.

1. Access Outlook's Calendar tool.
2. View next month's calendar using the Month button (31) on the Standard toolbar and the vertical scroll bar.
3. Create a New Recurring Appointment for the first Monday of next month. Your appointment time starts at 7:30 AM and ends at 8:00 AM.
4. Select a weekly Recurrence pattern that will recur every week on Monday, and will end after 3 occurrences.
5. Enter **Marcie's Highlighting Course** in the *Subject* text box.
6. Select a reminder that will occur 5 minutes prior to the commencement of the course.
7. Save and close the Recurring Appointment dialog box.
8. Customize your calendar to display only Monday, Tuesday, and Wednesday in the workweek. The start time for each workweek day is 6:45 AM and the end time is 3:00 PM.
9. Change your calendar's background color to green and then save your changes.
10. Display your calendar using the Work Week view and notice your customized changes.
11. Print your calendar using the Monthly Style, displaying your three recurring appointments.
12. Once you have successfully printed your calendar, delete the recurring appointment and return your calendar to its original settings (yellow background, with a Monday through Friday workweek, 8:00 AM to 5:00 PM each day).

OUTLOOK

2.7.4 Armstrong Equipment Rental: Managing Outlook Information

In this exercise, you practice creating new tasks and contacts, creating a new category, assigning contacts and tasks to categories, and finding and printing all Outlook items related to a specific category.

1. Use the Tasks tool to add the following two new tasks:
   - Enter 3 new Garden Equipment Distributors to contacts list
   - Create "Garden Equipment" category
2. Since you will be starting and completing both tasks today, specify today's date in the *Due date* and *Start date* drop-down lists.
3. For the first task, add a reminder to occur 5 minutes from now.
4. Use the Contacts tool to add the following new garden equipment distributors:

   George Alexander
   Job Title: **Sales Manager**
   Company: **Fonda Power Products**
   Address: **2810 - 10th Avenue**
   Rutland, Vermont
   70452

   Hanna Balcomb
   Job Title: **Marketing Representative**
   Company: **Webber Chain Saws**
   Address: **Box 300**
   Manchester, New Hampshire
   82571

   Duncan MacKenzie
   Job Title: **Owner**
   Company: **Evergo Lawnmowers**
   Address: **47 Waterville Way**
   Lewiston, Maine
   65993
5. While displaying your contacts list using the Detailed Address Cards view, highlight one contact by clicking on it once. Use the Edit, Categories menu command to create a new category called "Garden Equipment."
6. Ensure that your contacts list is displaying. Assign each of the new contacts created in step 4 to the "Garden Equipment" category.

7. Assign both of the tasks created in step 1 to the "Garden Equipment" category.
8. Use the By Category view to display your task list.
9. Use the Advanced Find command to locate all the Outlook items that have been assigned to the "Garden Equipment" category.
10. Once the Find results are displaying in the Advanced Find dialog box, use the File, Print menu command to print a copy of the results. Select the Table Style in the *Print style* area.
11. While viewing your task list, mark the tasks from step 1 as completed.
12. As a final step, reset your Master Category List.

2.7.5 On Your Own: Creating and Printing a Practice Schedule

As a famous and extremely busy actor, enter all of your appointments for next week in your Outlook calendar. Your appointments will include visiting a hospital, talking to a local high school, practicing for an upcoming movie, visiting your eye doctor, and being the guest speaker at a charity benefit. Your calendar should also include one recurring event, an autograph signing session, which takes place for three days of this week at 6:30 PM. While displaying your calendar using the Week button, add several tasks that relate to your appointments using your TaskPad. To customize your print settings, use the Page Setup command to include the TaskPad on the printed page. Print a copy of this busy Calendar week using your customized Weekly style. Finally save your busy week as a Web page entitled "Hollywood Week."

2.7.6 On Your Own: Populating Your Calendar

Delete any items from your Outlook calendar that you added in this chapter. Populate the next few months of your Outlook calendar with real appointments and events and then print it out.

2.8 Case Problems: Furniture Source

Kristen Grady is starting to feel overwhelmed by her extra responsibilities. She knows that if she could deal with day-to-day information with greater ease, she would be able to tackle the other challenging duties of her position. As a result, Kristen has decided to transfer all calendar- and task-related details to Outlook.

In the following case problems, assume the role of Kristen and perform the same steps that she identifies. You may want to re-read the chapter opening before proceeding.

1. After working through this learning guide, Kristen feels ready to tackle that mound of paper notes on her desk. But first, she wants to customize the Outlook bar to her needs. She decides to add the following new folders to the My Shortcuts group in the Outlook Bar:

Group name	*Folder name*	*Folder contents*
My Shortcuts	Business Contacts	Contact Items
	Don't Forget	Task Items
	Sales Meetings	Appointment Items

2. One by one, Kristen begins going through the scraps of paper on her desk and enters the information on them in Outlook. One scrap of paper has Helena Richards' contact information on it. Kristen adds the information to her "Business Contacts" folder. Helena, a local sales representative, works from the following address: **21102 Ownby Lane, Incline Village, Nevada 89450**. Her telephone number is **702-111-1111** and her e-mail address is **hrichards@provider.com**.

   Many of the notes on her desk describe tasks that she has yet to perform. Kristen types the following tasks into the "Don't Forget" folder:
   —Create the schedule for the regional sales meeting and send it to the reps.
   —Compile data for the upcoming sales meeting.
   —Add business contact information to the "Business Contacts" folder.

   After tossing all the notes that have been cluttering her desk into the garbage can, Kristen is starting to feel in control.

3. Upon returning to the office after a meeting with Helena Richards, Kristen displays the contents of her "Don't Forget" folder. One task in particular blares out at her: *Create the schedule for the regional sales meeting and send it to the reps.* With a shrug, she decides that she can't put this task off any longer.

   Kristen switches to her "Sales Meetings" folder and enters the events listed below. (*Note:* The sales meeting is next week!)

Thursday	9 AM	Introduction: By Kristen Grady
	10 AM	Topic: Product Development
	Noon	Lunch
	1 PM	Topic: New Product Lines
	2 PM	Topic: The Competition
	4 PM	Softball!
Friday	9 AM	Topic: Planning for the Future
	Noon	Lunch
	1 PM	Topic: Current Sales Figures
	2–4 PM	Topic: Our New Partners
	6 PM	Barbecue and Country Dance
Saturday	7–9 AM	Farewell breakfast

   She then prints a copy of the schedule in the Weekly Style and prepares to send a copy to each of the representatives in her region.

4. After completing the task in exercise 3, Kristen opens her "Don't Forget" folder and crosses the "Create the schedule for the regional sales meeting and send it to the reps" task off the list. She then prints a revised task list.

   Kristen receives an e-mail message from the Furniture Source president, Alphonso Banks, suggesting that the Sales Meeting schedule be posted to the Internet. Eager to impress her boss, Kristen saves next week's Sales Meeting schedule as a Web page named "Meeting," specifying "Regional Sales Meeting" as the calendar title. Amazed that she can now see her desktop, Kristen sighs with relief as she exits Outlook 2000.

   Important: Since the folders you created in this case study were for instructional purposes only, refer to the instructions at the end of Lesson 2.3.3 to remove the three folders you created in this case study.

NOTES

Microsoft Outlook 2000
Working with E-Mail

CHAPTER THREE

Chapter Outline

Learning Objectives

After reading this chapter, you will be able to:

- Address, compose, and flag messages
- Work with attachments
- View, print, reply to, and forward messages
- Embellish and manage your mail
- Create Office documents from within Outlook, and share mail and contact data

Case Study

Sleepy Hollow Community Center

Mary Rexroat has been working hard to bring a dream to reality. A longtime resident of Sleepy Hollow, she is trying to raise money to build a new community center. Plans for the new center include a swimming pool, a dance hall, a workout facility, a huge ballroom, a couple of baseball fields, a soccer field, a radio station, an art room, and a lot more. To pay for the new center, which will cost millions, Mary sends out handwritten letters to the town's residents asking for donations. Although she believes that the personal touch inherent in handwritten letters can be effective in raising money, her pen is slowing her down. As a result, although she'll still use handwritten letters to establish initial contact with donors, she would like to use e-mail whenever possible to respond to any inquiries that she receives.

In this chapter, you and Mary learn how to use Outlook 2000's mail features. You learn how to prepare outgoing mail, handle incoming mail, manage your mail, and integrate Outlook 2000 with existing Office applications and other Outlook tools.

3.1 Preparing the Student Data Files

Before you can send and receive e-mail, you need two types of software. First, you need software such as Outlook for composing and managing e-mail messages. Second, you need software for transporting your e-mail to and from other people over the Internet. This latter task can be performed by your Internet Service Provider (ISP), by your online service such as The Microsoft Network or America Online, or by a program such as Microsoft Exchange Server stored on your office network.

Important: *We assume that you have access to software for getting your e-mail to where you want it to go and that you have a valid e-mail address. If this isn't the case, you can still perform many of the steps in this chapter, however, you won't be able to send and receive mail. Also, in this guide, we refer to the files that have been created for you as the* ***student data files***. *Depending on your computer or lab setup, these files may be located on a floppy diskette, in a folder on your hard disk, or on a network server. If necessary, ask your instructor or lab assistant where to find these data files. To download the Advantage Series' student data files from the Internet, visit McGraw-Hill's Information Technology Web site at:*

http://www.mhhe.com/it

You will also need to identify a personal storage location for the files that you create, modify, and save.

3.1.1 Creating a Message Folder

FEATURE
As your incoming messages start to collect in your Inbox, it is advisable to organize them in folders. After you've created a new folder, you can easily drag and drop messages into it.

METHOD
1. CHOOSE: File, Folder, New
2. TYPE: a name for the folder in the *Folder name* text box
3. SELECT: the location for the new folder

PRACTICE
In this lesson, you create a folder for storing your student data files. You will use these files for practice throughout this chapter.

Setup: Ensure that Outlook is loaded on your computer.

1 To create a new folder:
CHOOSE: File, New, Folder

2 To give the new folder a name:
TYPE: **Student Data Files** in the *Folder name* text box

3 To store mail items in the folder:
SELECT: Mail Items from the *Folder contains* drop-down list

4 To store the new folder in the Inbox folder:
CLICK: Inbox () in the list box
CLICK: OK command button
CLICK: Yes command button if prompted about adding a shortcut to the Outlook Bar

5 To prepare for the next lesson, let's display the contents of the Student Data Files folder.
CLICK: My Shortcuts group button
CLICK: Student Data Files icon () in the Outlook Bar
No messages are displaying in the Information Viewer area because the folder is empty.

6 Continue to the next lesson.

3.1.2 Copying the Student Data Files

PRACTICE
To prepare for working through the modules in this chapter, this lesson leads you through copying several practice messages to your Student Data Files folder.

Setup: Ensure that you've completed the last lesson and that the Student Data Files folder is displaying. Also, make sure that you know the location of your student data files.

1 In this step, you're going to launch the program Windows Explorer for copying several practice files to your Student Data Files folder. To launch Windows Explorer:
CLICK: Start button on the Windows taskbar
CHOOSE: Programs, Windows Explorer

2 Maximize the Windows Explorer window by clicking its Maximize button (). Figure 3.1 provides an example of the Windows Explorer window.

Figure 3.1
Windows Explorer

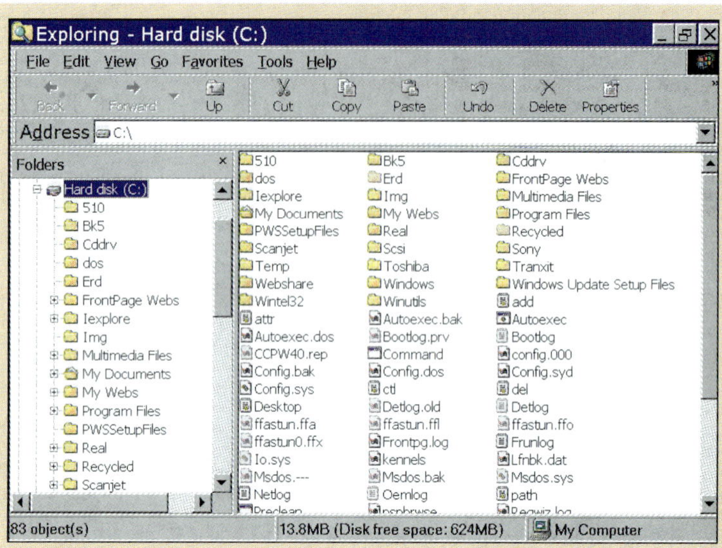

3 The contents of your computer's hard disk should be displaying in the left pane of the Explorer window. Depending on whether your student data files are stored on your computer's hard disk or on a floppy diskette, perform one of the following two procedures to navigate to those files:

- *If your student data files are stored on the hard disk*: Navigate to the files by double-clicking folders located in the left pane. Your student data files should now be displaying in the right pane.
- *If your student data files are stored on a diskette*: Navigate to the files by double-clicking the 3½ Floppy (A:) icon in the left pane. (*Note:* You will probably have to drag the left pane's vertical scroll bar upward before you can see the 3½ Floppy (A:) icon.) Your student data files should now be displaying in the right pane.

4 Now, to view both the Outlook and Windows Explorer windows on the screen at the same time, do the following:
RIGHT-CLICK: an empty part of the Windows taskbar
CHOOSE: Tile Vertically
Your screen should now appear similar, but not identical, to Figure 3.2.

Figure 3.2
Tiling windows

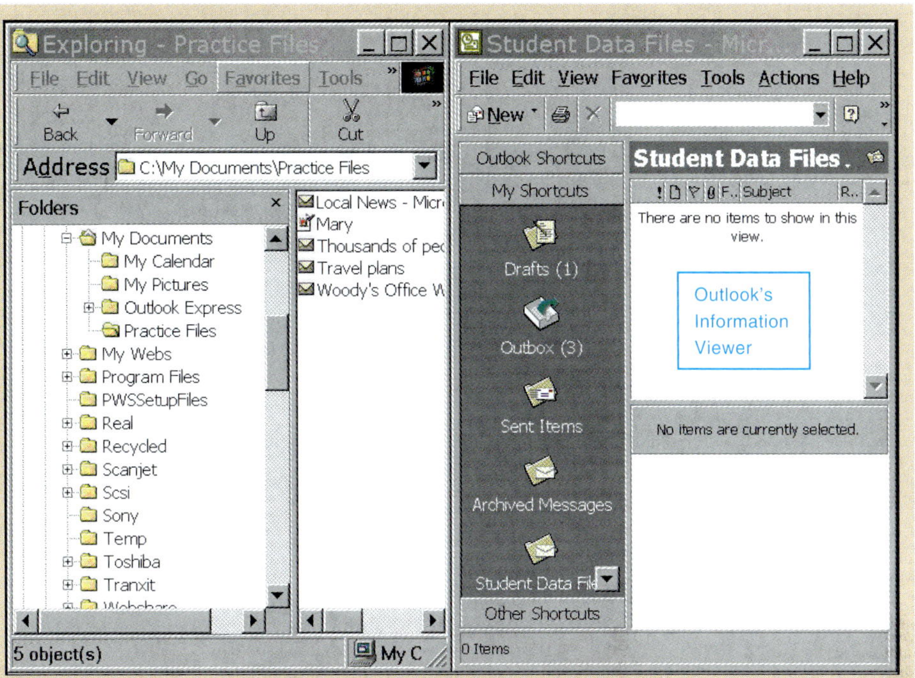

5 Each message file is represented by a mail icon (✉). To select all the messages stored in the Explorer window:
CLICK: the first message item in the list
PRESS: CTRL and hold it down
CLICK: the remaining message files
Four messages should now be selected.

6 To copy the selected files to your Student Data Files folder, do the following:
DRAG: the selected messages to the Information Viewer area in the Outlook window

7 Close the Windows Explorer window by clicking its Close button (☒).

8 Maximize the Outlook window. Your screen should now appear similar to Figure 3.3.

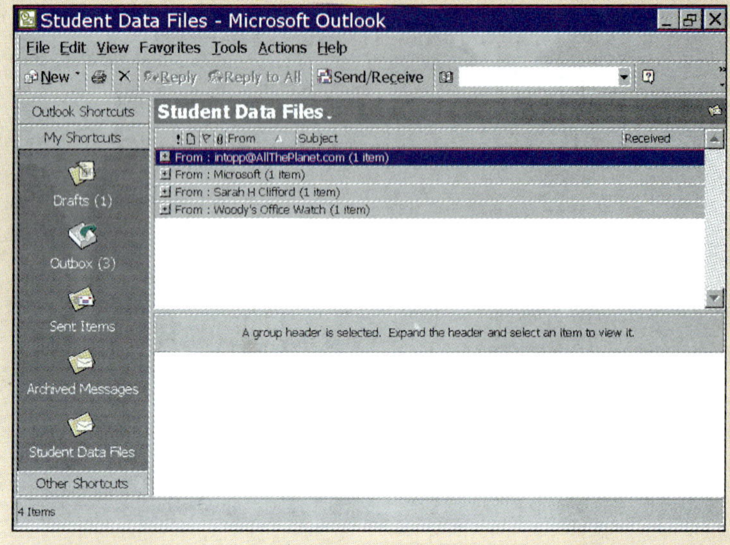

Figure 3.3
Copied messages appear in the Student Data Files folder

3.1 Self Check What two types of software do you need before you can send and receive e-mail?

3.2 Preparing Outgoing Messages

Once e-mail software such as Microsoft Outlook has been installed on your computer and you have access to software for transporting your e-mail over the Internet, you can begin sending and receiving e-mail. In this module, we describe what to know about addressing and composing messages, attaching files, flagging messages, and delivering messages to others.

3.2.1 Addressing and Composing Messages

FEATURE

The process of addressing a message involves specifying your recipient's e-mail address and typing in a few words that your recipient will use to identify your message. You can type in your recipient's e-mail address directly or access it from your contact list. E-mail addresses consist of a user name, followed by @, followed by a domain name. For example, in the e-mail address *shutchinson@msn.com, shutchinson* is the user name and *msn.com* is the domain name. To send a message to multiple recipients, separate each mail address with a semicolon (;).

METHOD

To start a new mail message and address it by typing:

1. CLICK: Inbox icon ( ) in the Outlook Bar
2. CLICK: New Mail Message button (New)
3. CLICK: in the *To* or *Cc* text box
4. TYPE: **an e-mail address**

To start a new mail message and address it using addresses stored in your contact list:

1. CLICK: Inbox icon ( ) in the Outlook Bar
2. CLICK: New Mail Message button (New)
3. CLICK: To or Cc command button
4. SELECT: *a name from the list box*
5. CLICK: To or Cc command button to insert the name as a message recipient
6. Optionally, repeat steps 4–5 to include additional message recipients.
7. CLICK: OK command button

PRACTICE

In this lesson, you will address and compose an e-mail message to yourself.

Setup: Ensure that Outlook is loaded.

1 To begin a new message:
CLICK: Inbox icon ( ) in the Outlook Bar
CLICK: New Mail Message button (New) on the Standard toolbar
The insertion point is blinking in the *To* text box and your screen should now appear similar to Figure 3.4.

OUTLOOK

Figure 3.4
Message window

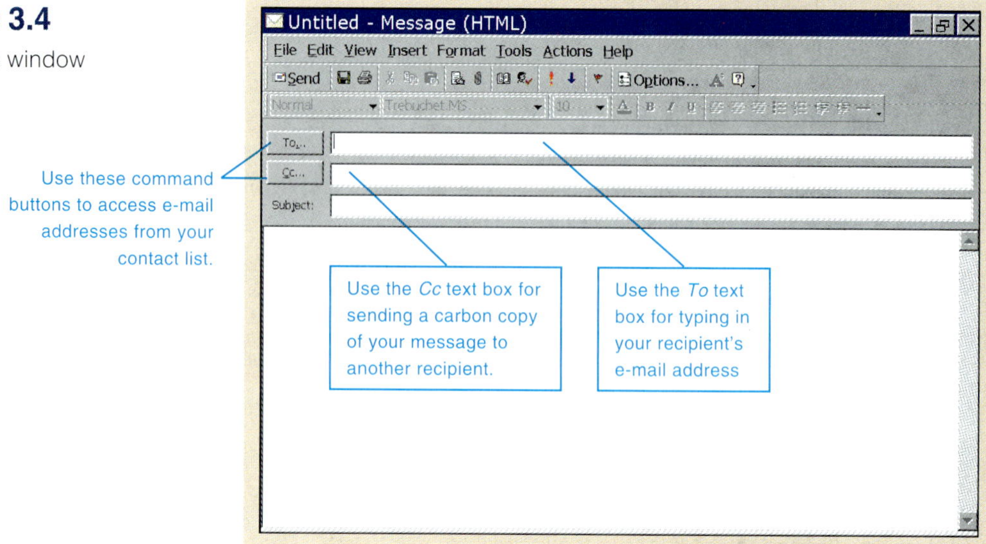

2 Let's send this first message to yourself.
TYPE: **your e-mail address** in the *To* text box

3 Let's say we want to send a carbon copy of the message to someone else. To copy the desired e-mail address from your contact list:
CLICK: Cc command button
The Select Names dialog box should now appear, an example of which appears in Figure 3.5.

Figure 3.5
Select Names dialog box

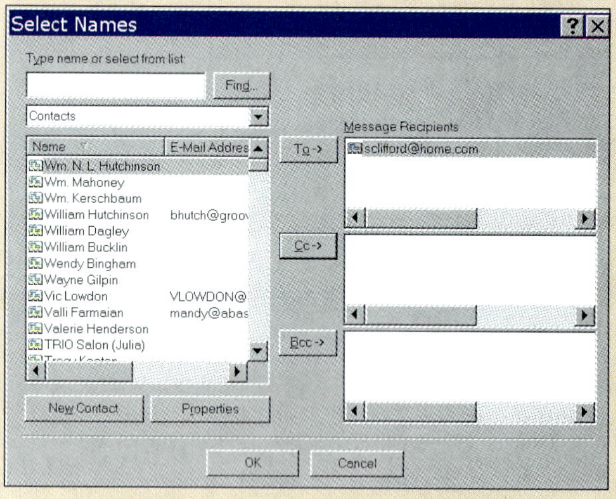

4 SELECT: any name in the list box on the left that has an associated e-mail address
CLICK: Cc command button, located in the middle of the dialog box
CLICK: OK command button
Note that names, not e-mail addresses, may now appear in the *To* and *Cc* text boxes. When you actually send the message, Outlook will automatically include the correct e-mail addresses.

5 Before continuing, let's remove the recipient from the *Cc* text box. To do so:
CLICK: in the *Cc* text box
PRESS: DELETE

6 To complete the *Subject* text box, do the following:
CLICK: in the *Subject* text box
TYPE: **Test Message**

7 To prepare for composing a message:
CLICK: in the large text area
Using the Formatting toolbar, you can format your messages with special fonts and sizes and with varied paragraph formatting affecting alignment and indentation. You can even format a message with color and bullets! If your recipient's e-mail program does not support message formatting, the received message will appear as plain text.

8 To type a message, do the following:
TYPE: **Reminder:**
PRESS: ENTER twice
TYPE: **To learn more about using Outlook 2000, check out the Outlook 2000 Home page at www.microsoft.com/office/outlook.**
PRESS: ENTER
Note that Outlook automatically formatted the Web address as a hyperlink. Your recipient can simply click the link to launch his or her browser software and go directly to the Web site. (*Note:* To edit a Web address, hold down CTRL and select the portion that you want to edit. Then make your changes.) Your screen should now appear similar to Figure 3.6.

Figure 3.6
Composing a message to yourself

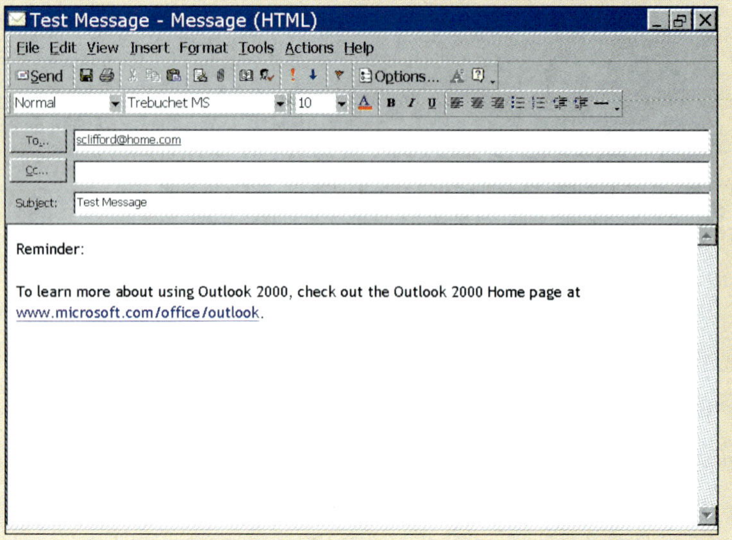

9 Keep the current message open for use in the next lesson.

3.2.2 Sending and Receiving Mail

FEATURE
By default, when you click the Send button in the message window, your message is saved to your Outbox folder. You must then click the Send and Receive button on the Standard toolbar to send your message to your recipient's mailbox. Received messages are represented by a mail icon ( ) on the taskbar.

METHOD
1. CLICK: Send button to save your message to your Outbox folder
2. CLICK: Send/Receive button to deliver messages located in your Outbox folder and to receive mail

PRACTICE
In this lesson, you send the e-mail message that you composed to yourself in the last lesson.

Setup: Ensure that you've completed the previous lesson in this module and that the Test Message window is displaying.

1 To send the message:
CLICK: Send button on the Standard toolbar
The Message window should have closed automatically.

2. To view your message in the Outbox folder:
CLICK: My Shortcuts group button on the Outlook Bar
CLICK: Outbox icon ( )
Your message should appear in the message list.

3. To deliver your message to yourself:
CLICK: Send and Receive button on the Standard toolbar

4. You should now be able to see a copy of the message you just sent in the Sent Items folder. Let's take a look.
CLICK: My Shortcuts group button in the Outlook Bar
CLICK: Sent Items icon ( )
Your message should appear in the list of sent items.

5. Before continuing:
CLICK: Outlook Shortcuts group button in the Outlook Bar
CLICK: Inbox icon ( ) in the Outlook Bar

6. If you don't yet see a mail icon ( ) next to your taskbar clock, then you'll have to click the Send and Receive button again to download the message that you sent to yourself. We now assume that a mail icon ( ) appears on the taskbar, indicating that the message was downloaded to your computer. You should also be able to see the message in the Information Viewer area (see below). We describe the different columns in the Information Viewer area in more detail in Module 3.3.

Messages that you haven't yet read appear in bold letters.

7. Continue to the next lesson.

3.2.3 Inserting Attachments

FEATURE
An easy way to share a file with friends and co-workers is to insert it as an attachment to your e-mail message.

METHOD
1. CLICK: Insert File button ( ) on the Standard toolbar, or CHOOSE: Insert, File
2. Navigate to where the attachment file is located
3. DOUBLE-CLICK: the attachment file

PRACTICE

You will now attach an existing file to a new mail message.

Setup: Ensure that you've completed the previous lessons in this module.

1. To begin a new mail message:
   CLICK: New Mail Message button (New) on the Standard toolbar

2. The insertion point is blinking in the *To* text field.
   TYPE: ***the e-mail addresses of several friends***, separating each address with a semicolon (no spaces allowed)
   (*Note:* If desired, you can substitute your e-mail address in the *To* text box.)

3. To complete the *Subject* text box, do the following:
   CLICK: in the *Subject* text box
   TYPE: **Class Project**

4. To type a message, do the following:
   CLICK: in the large text box
   TYPE: **Hi everyone! For a class project, I'm attaching a photo of Baby Mary. She's the daughter of the person who wrote the book I'm using. Right now, I'm learning how to insert attachments in e-mail messages. Hope to see you soon! *your name***

5. To attach the photo:
   CLICK: Insert File button ( ) on the Standard toolbar

6. Using the Insert File dialog box, navigate to where your student files are located.

7. To insert the file in the message:
   DOUBLE-CLICK: "Mary" graphic file
   Your screen should now appear similar to Figure 3.7.

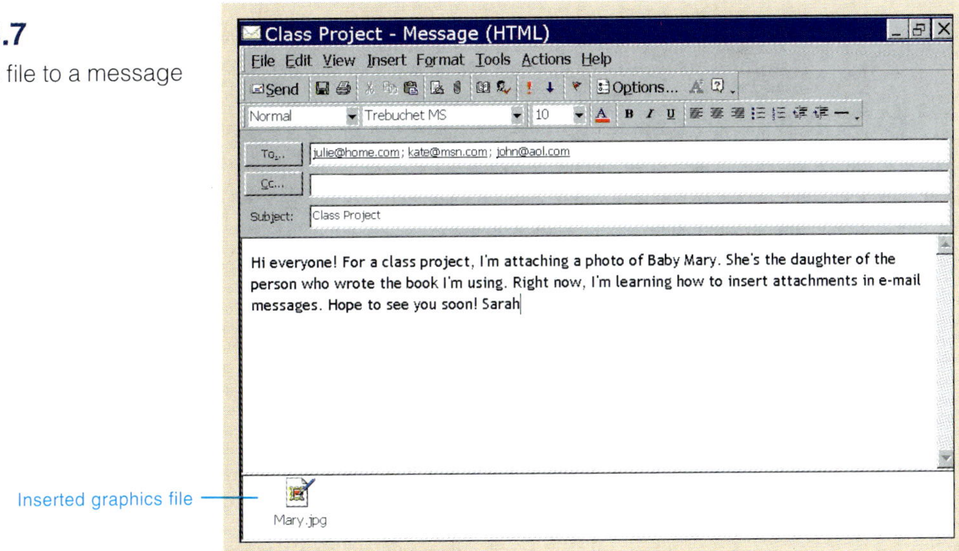

Figure 3.7
Attaching a file to a message

8. Continue to the next lesson.

3.2.4 Flagging Messages

FEATURE

By flagging messages, you provide recipients with additional information and reminders relating to your message. For example, you can add a flag to your message that says "For Your Information" or "No Response Necessary." Or you can add a flag requesting that your recipient reply to or read a message by a certain date. Messages that have been flagged display with a flag (🚩) in the Flag Status column in the Information Viewer.

METHOD

1. CLICK: Flag for Follow Up button (🚩) on the Standard toolbar
2. SELECT: an option from the *Flag to* drop-down list
3. SELECT: a date from the *Due by* drop-down list, when appropriate
4. CLICK: OK command button

PRACTICE

You will now flag a message for follow-up and also assign an importance level.

Setup: Ensure that you've completed the previous lessons in this module and that the Class Project message is displaying.

1. Let's assign a flag to the open message.
   CLICK: Flag for Follow Up button ( ) on the Standard toolbar
   The Flag for Follow Up dialog box should now appear (Figure 3.8).

Figure 3.8
Flag for Follow Up dialog box

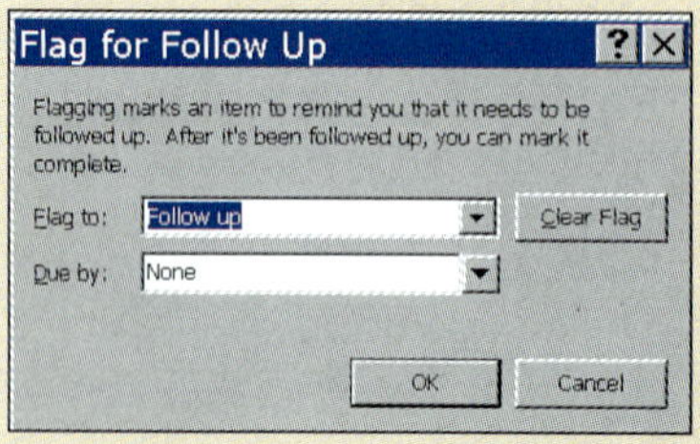

2. CLICK: *Flag to* drop-down arrow
   CHOOSE: No Response Necessary from the drop-down list
   CLICK: OK command button
   Note that the flagged information appears at the top of the message window.

3. Using a separate procedure, you can also assign a high or low importance level to your messages. By default, messages are assigned a normal importance level. In your recipient's Inbox folder, important messages are easily spotted because they're flagged with an exclamation mark (!). Lower priority messages, on the other hand, are flagged with a down arrow (↓). Let's assign a low importance level to this message.
   CLICK: Importance: Low button ( ) on the Standard toolbar

4. To send the file:
   CLICK: Send button on the Standard toolbar

5. On your own, display the contents of your Outbox folder. The Class Project message should appear similar, but not identical, to the following:

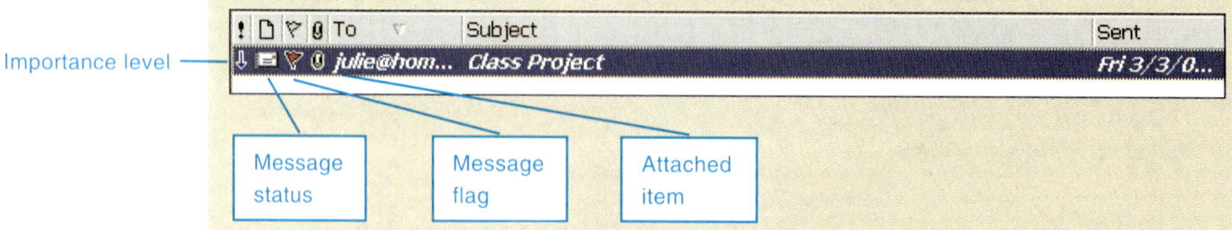

6. To delete the message from your Outbox folder:
   CLICK: the message, if it isn't selected already
   CLICK: Delete button ( ) on the Standard toolbar

3.2 Self Check When might you want to add a flag to a message?

3.3 Handling Incoming Messages

Outlook notifies you in several different ways when you've received mail. First, as mentioned previously, a mail icon ( ) will display next to the taskbar clock when new mail arrives. Second, if you look in the Outlook Bar, the number in parentheses next to the Inbox icon tells you how many messages you've received that you haven't yet read. Third, in the Information Viewer, the titles of unread messages appear in bold letters. Finally, if your computer is always connected to the Internet, as is the case with cable and most network connections, a dialog box may display indicating that you've received mail. In this module, we introduce several techniques for handling received messages.

3.3.1 Viewing and Navigating Mail

FEATURE

When the Inbox tool is active, the Information Viewer uses several columns to identify incoming mail. From left to right, the first few columns help to identify a message's importance level, the type of message, whether the message has been flagged with a follow-up message, and whether the message includes a file attachment.

METHOD

1. To open and then navigate mail:
   CHOOSE: View, Current View, *option*
   DOUBLE-CLICK: a message title to read its content
   CLICK: Previous Item ( ) or Next Item ( ) button
   SELECT: an option from the drop-down list
2. To preview and then navigate mail:
   CHOOSE: View, Preview Pane
   PRESS: Space Bar to navigate your messages and message list

PRACTICE

In this lesson, you practice changing the current view, reading mail, and navigating your message list.

Setup: Ensure that Outlook is loaded and that you prepared the student data files in Module 3.1.

OUTLOOK

1 Because it is used to store mail messages, the Student Data Files folder that you created in the beginning of this chapter works the same as your Inbox folder. So that we're working with the same files, we're going to use the Student Data Files folder throughout this module.
CLICK: My Shortcuts group button in the Outlook Bar
CLICK: Student Data Files icon ( ) in the Outlook Bar
Because we copied the messages in the Student Data Files folder into Outlook, Outlook automatically grouped the messages by their sender. Note that each group contains one item.

2 By default, Outlook lists your messages using the Messages view. Let's change the current view.
CHOOSE: View, Current View, Messages with AutoPreview
Your screen should now appear similar to Figure 3.9. Table 3.1 lists several icons that are used to identify messages in the Information Viewer area.

Figure 3.9
Inbox folder column headings

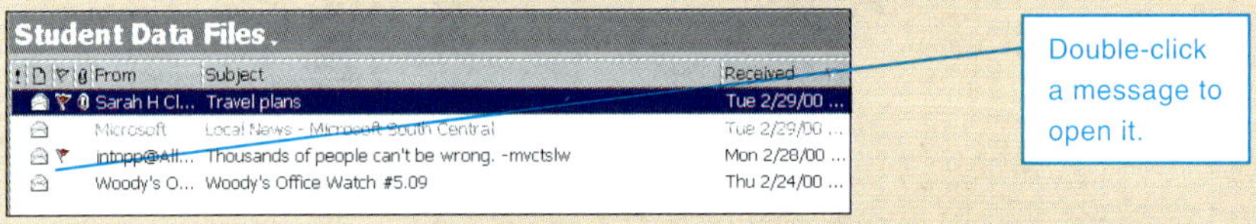

Table 3.1
Message icons

Icon	Description
	High priority
	Low priority
	Unread message
	Read message
	The sender replied to this message
	The sender attached a reminder to the message
	Attachment

3 Right now the preview pane is displaying. To remove the preview pane:
CHOOSE: View, Preview Pane

4 To redisplay the preview pane:
CHOOSE: View, Preview Pane

5 You can scroll the contents of the preview pane by clicking the Space Bar. To illustrate:
PRESS: Space Bar
With each press of the Space Bar, the text in the preview window scrolls upward.

6 PRESS: Space Bar four times to scroll to the bottom of the message
PRESS: Space Bar once more to preview the next message

7 To close the preview pane:
CHOOSE: View, Preview Pane

8 Let's open an existing message.
DOUBLE-CLICK: the message from Microsoft
Your screen should now appear similar to Figure 3.10.

Figure 3.10
Opening a received message

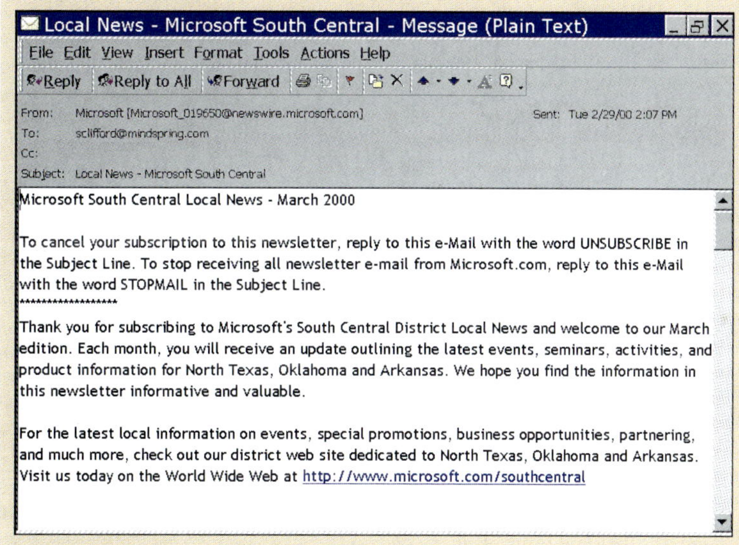

9 Rather than open the other messages in your mail folder by double-clicking, as in step 8, you can navigate to them using buttons on the Standard toolbar. To illustrate:
CLICK: Previous Item button (▲▾), not its drop-down arrow, on the Standard toolbar
The previous message in the message list should now be displaying.

10 CLICK: Next Item button (▼▾), not its drop-down arrow, on the Standard toolbar
The message from Microsoft reappears.

OUTLOOK

11 CLICK: Next Item button ( ) on the Standard toolbar
The next message in the message list is displaying.

12 CLICK: Previous Item ( ) drop-down arrow
Your screen should now appear similar to Figure 3.11. This menu is particularly helpful when your message list gets long.

Figure 3.11

Navigating your message list

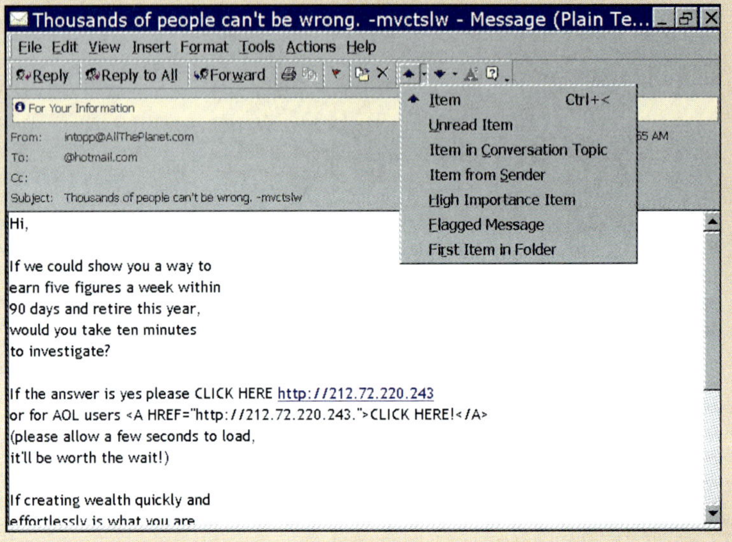

13 CHOOSE: Flagged Message from the drop-down menu
The first flagged message in your message list should be displaying.

14 To close the current message:
CLICK: its Close button ( )

15 Continue to the next lesson.

3.3.2 Printing Mail

FEATURE
It's sometimes easier to read e-mail messages in printed form, especially when they are really long. In Outlook, the procedure for printing is the same as when using other Office 2000 applications.

METHOD
1. To print a message:
   CHOOSE: File, Print, or
   CLICK: Print button ( ) on the Standard toolbar
2. To change the current print settings:
   CHOOSE: File, Print
   CLICK: Page Setup command button
   CLICK: Print command button after making selections
   CLICK: OK command button

PRACTICE
In this lesson, you print a message stored in your Student Data Files folder.

Setup: Ensure that you've completed the previous lesson and that the contents of your Student Data Files folder is displaying.

1 To print the "Thousands of people can't be wrong" message stored in the Student Data Files folder, do the following:
CLICK: "Thousands of people..." message in the Information Viewer
CHOOSE: File, Print
The Print dialog box will appear (Figure 3.12). Note that "Memo Style" is selected in the *Print style* area.

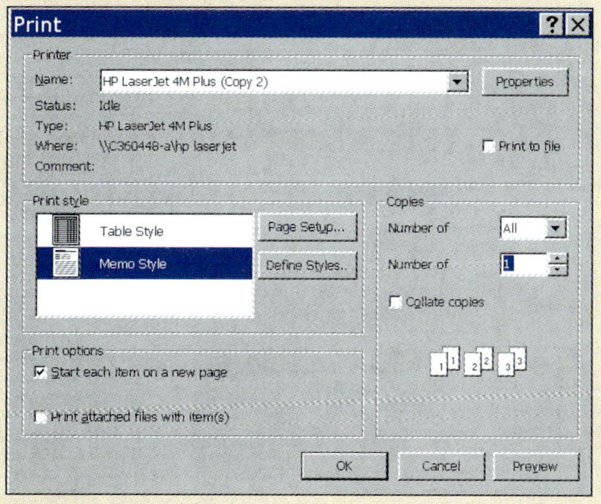

Figure 3.12
Print dialog box

2. Let's preview the current message using the Memo Style:
CLICK: Preview command button

3. To zoom in closer:
CLICK: near the top of the message
Your screen should now appear similar to Figure 3.13. Note that this message contains a flag, as described in the message header.

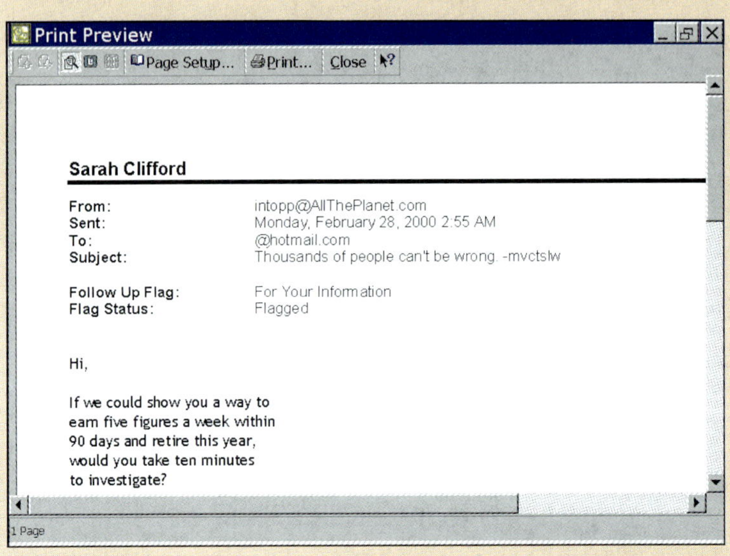

Figure 3.13
Previewing a message using the Memo style

4. To return to the Print dialog box:
CLICK: Print button (🖨) in the toolbar

5. To customize the settings associated with the Memo Style:
CLICK: Page Setup command button
The Page Setup dialog box should now appear (Figure 3.14). The *Format* tab is used for customizing fonts and shading, the *Paper* tab is used for selecting an alternate paper type and customizing the margin settings, and the *Header/Footer* tab is used for specifying a header or footer.

Figure 3.14
Page Setup dialog box

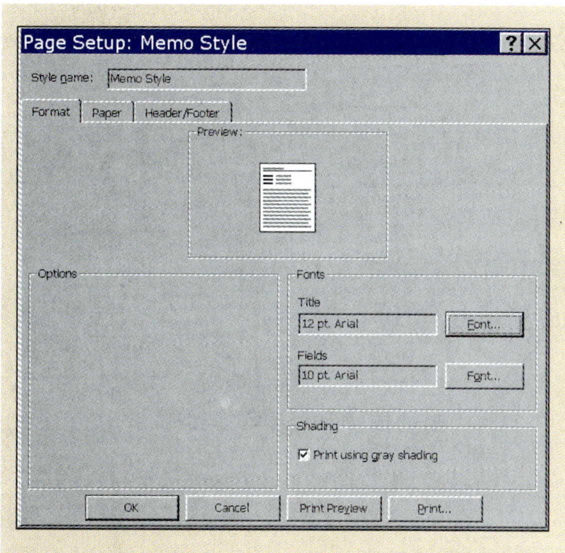

6 Let's leave this dialog box without making any selections.
CLICK: OK command button

7 To proceed with printing the message:
CLICK: OK command button

3.3.3 Replying to and Forwarding Mail

FEATURE

When you receive a message, you will often want to reply to the author of the message. Rather than beginning a new message, you can easily use the Reply button ( ) in the Message window. The new message is automatically addressed to the original sender and includes a copy of the original message. If the original message was sent to numerous recipients, the Reply to All button ( ) will automatically create a new message to the sender and to each of the original recipients. When you think a message that you've received would be of interest to someone else, consider forwarding a copy of the message using the Forward button ( ). As with replying, forwarding includes a copy of the original message in the new message.

METHOD

1. Open the message you want to reply to or forward.
2. CLICK: Reply button ( ), Reply to All button ( ), or the Forward button ( )

PRACTICE

You will now practice replying to and forwarding messages.

Setup: Ensure that you've completed the previous lessons in this module and that the contents of your Student Data Files folder are displaying.

1. Let's open the Microsoft message item.
   DOUBLE-CLICK: Microsoft message item

2. Let's see what happens when we click the Reply button ( ) on the Standard Buttons toolbar.
   CLICK: Reply button ( )

3. Maximize the message window. Your screen should now appear similar to Figure 3.15. Note that the sender's e-mail address, in this case Microsoft's, appears in the *To* text box and that a copy of the original message is displaying in the message area. When replying to messages, you type your reply at the insertion point located above the original message.

Figure 3.15
Replying to a message

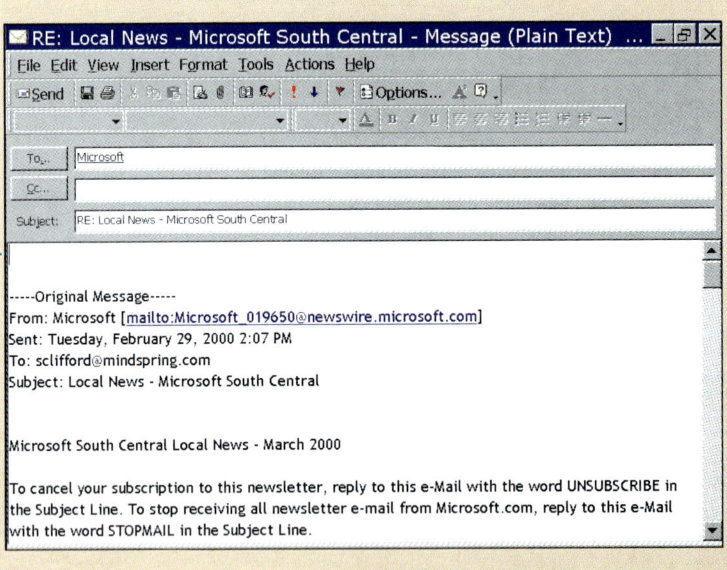

4. To close the message window without sending the message:
   CLICK: its Close button ( )

5. Let's see what happens when we click the Forward button ( ) on the Standard Buttons toolbar.
   CLICK: Forward button ( )
   Your screen looks the same as when replying to a message, except that you must insert an e-mail address in the *To* text box. You might also want to include some remarks above the message in the message window, explaining why you're forwarding the message.

6. To close the message window without sending the message:
CLICK: its Close button (☒)

7. On your own, close the original message from Microsoft.

3.3.4 Opening and Saving Attached Files

FEATURE

When you open attached files, they open into the application that was used to create them, or *source application*. For example, if you open a Microsoft Word attachment, it will open into Microsoft Word. An Excel attachment will open into Microsoft Excel, and so on. If the necessary source application isn't stored on your computer, you will receive an error message.

METHOD

1. To open the attached file:
   DOUBLE-CLICK: the attachment
   CHOOSE: *Open it* option button
   CLICK: OK command button
2. To save an attached file:
   RIGHT-CLICK: the attachment
   CHOOSE: Save As from the right-click menu

PRACTICE

In this lesson, you open and then save a file attachment.

Setup: Ensure that you've completed the previous lessons in this module and that the contents of your Student Data Files folder are displaying.

1. The "Travel Plans" message contains an attached file.
DOUBLE-CLICK: "Travel Plans" message

2. Let's open the attached file.
DOUBLE-CLICK: attachment icon located at the bottom of the message window
The dialog box in Figure 3.16 should now appear. Note that the *Save it to disk* option button is selected.

Figure 3.16

Opening Mail Attachment dialog box

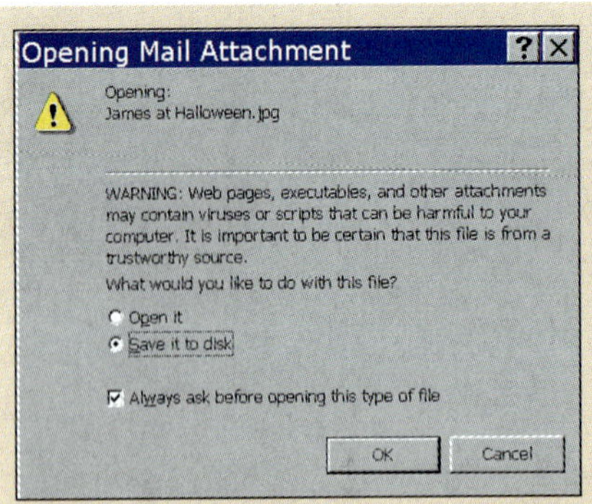

3 Rather than save the file to disk, let's open the file.
SELECT: *Open it* option button
CLICK: OK command button
Your screen should now appear similar to Figure 3.17. The file, because it is a graphics file, automatically opened into an application called Microsoft Photo Editor. Using this application, you can edit or print the graphics file. If your file attachment had been a Microsoft Word file, for example, it would have opened into Microsoft Word.

Figure 3.17

Opening the mail attachment

4 To close Microsoft Photo Editor:
CLICK: its Close button (×)
The message window should reappear.

5 To save the file to disk:
RIGHT-CLICK: the file
CHOOSE: Save As from the right-click menu

6. Navigate to your personal storage location using the *Save in* drop-down list or the Places Bar.

7. Let's save the file using the existing name.
CLICK: Save command button

8. Close the message window.

3.3 Self Check What does it mean to *reply* to a message?

3.4 Taking Control

Now that you know how to send and retrieve mail, it's time to explore some useful techniques for embellishing and managing mail. In this module, you learn how to change the look of mail, add a signature to outgoing messages, keep your mail organized, and archive messages for long-term storage.

3.4.1 Customizing the Look of Mail

FEATURE
To change the appearance of your outgoing mail, you can select alternate fonts and sizes or change the overall look of your messages by applying one of Outlook's preexisting mail templates. Not only do mail templates apply different fonts to your messages, they also embellish your messages with colors and background pictures.

METHOD
- To change fonts for messages you compose:
  CHOOSE: Tools, Options
  CLICK: *Mail Format* tab
  CLICK: Fonts command button
  CLICK: OK command button after making font selections
- To apply a mail template to messages you compose:
  CHOOSE: Tools, Options
  CLICK: *Mail Format* tab
  CLICK: Stationery Picker command button
  SELECT: a stationery template in the *Stationery* list box
  CLICK: OK command button

PRACTICE

In this lesson, you practice changing fonts and applying a stationery template.

Setup: Ensure that Outlook is loaded and that you prepared the student data files in Module 3.1.

1. Let's change the fonts used for new messages.
CHOOSE: Tools, Options
CLICK: *Mail Format* tab
Your screen should now appear similar to Figure 3.18.

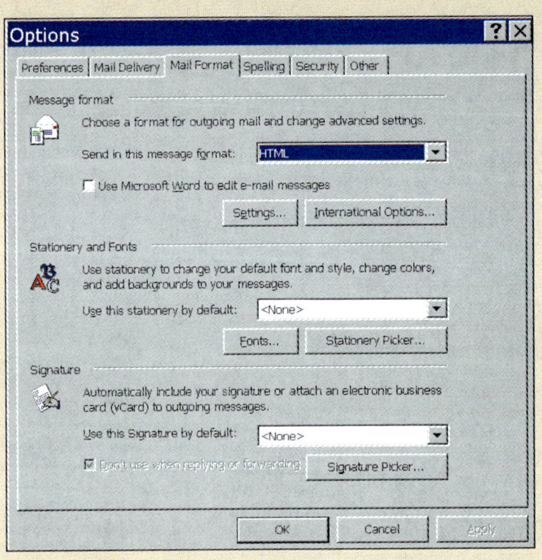

Figure 3.18
Options dialog box:
Mail Format tab

2. In the *Stationery and Fonts* area:
CLICK: Fonts command button
The Fonts dialog box should now appear (Figure 3.19). Using this dialog box, you can select what fonts to use when composing messages and when replying to and forwarding messages.

Figure 3.19

Fonts dialog box

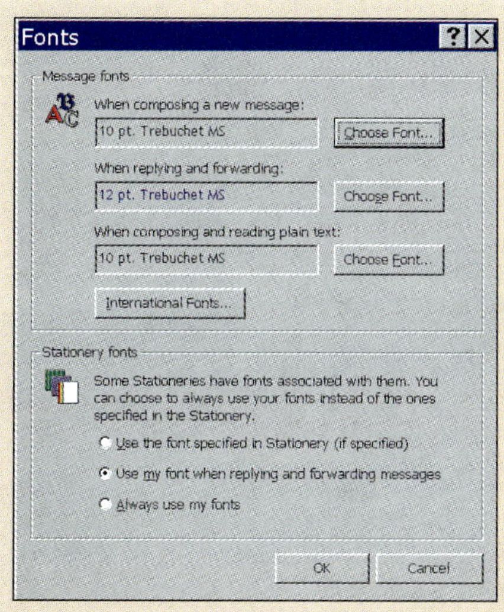

3 For practice, let's select an alternate font for new messages. Locate the Choose Font command button in the *When composing a new message* area.
CLICK: Choose Font command button (the first one)

4 To increase the font size:
SELECT: 16 in the *Size* list box
CLICK: OK command button

5 CLICK: OK to leave the Fonts dialog box
CLICK: OK to leave the Options dialog box

6 To start a new mail message and see the effect of your font change:
CLICK: New Mail Message button (New) on the Standard toolbar
CLICK: *in the large text area*
TYPE: **a few words**
Note the larger point size.

7 To close the message without saving:
CLICK: Close button (×) of the message window
CLICK: No command button

8 Let's apply a mail template to new messages.
CHOOSE: Tools, Options
CLICK: *Mail Format* tab
CLICK: Stationery Picker command button
The Stationery Picker dialog box should now appear (Figure 3.20).

Figure 3.20

Stationery Picker dialog box

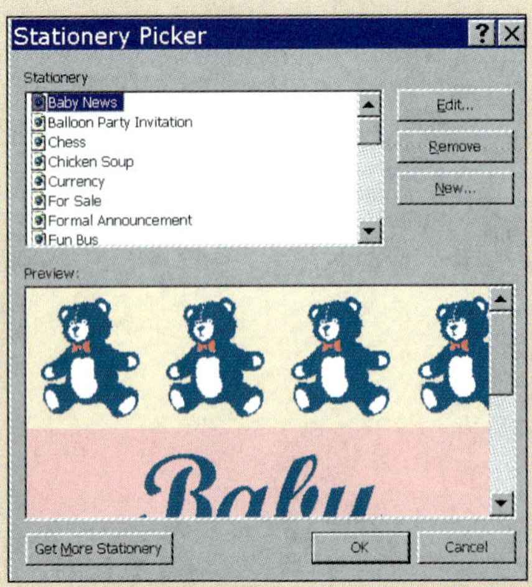

9 SELECT: "Fun Bus" template from the *Stationery* list box
CLICK: OK command button
CLICK: OK command button again to leave the Options dialog box

10 To start a new mail message and see the effect of mail template:
CLICK: New Mail Message button (New) on the Standard toolbar
Your screen should now appear similar to Figure 3.21.

Figure 3.21

Stationery Picker dialog box

11 To close the message without saving:
CLICK: Close button (☒) of the message window

12 Before continuing to the next lesson, let's undo your font and template changes.
CHOOSE: Tools, Options
CLICK: *Mail Format* tab
SELECT: <None> from the *Use this stationery by default* drop-down list
CLICK: Fonts command button
CLICK: the first Choose Font command button
SELECT: 10 in the *Size* list box
CLICK: OK command button
CLICK: OK command button to leave the Fonts dialog box
CLICK: OK command button to leave the Options dialog box

3.4.2 Creating a Signature

FEATURE

In Outlook, a *signature* is text that appears on the bottom of all your outgoing messages. A signature contains identifying information such as your full name, company name, e-mail address, Web address, or other information.

METHOD

1. CHOOSE: Tools, Options while displaying the Inbox folder
   CLICK: *Mail Format* tab
2. CLICK: Signature Picker command button
3. CLICK: New command button
4. TYPE: **a signature name** in the *Enter a name...* text box
5. CLICK: Next command button
6. TYPE: **your signature text** in the *Signature text* text box
7. CLICK: Finish command button
8. CLICK: OK twice to return to the Outlook window

PRACTICE

You will now create a new signature and then display it in a new message.

Setup: Ensure that you've completed the previous lessons in this module and that the contents of the Student Data Files folder are displaying.

1 Let's create a signature that contains your name and personal information. To begin:
CHOOSE: Tools, Options
CLICK: *Mail Format* tab
CLICK: Signature Picker command button
Your screen should now appear similar to Figure 3.22.

Figure 3.22
Signature Picker dialog box

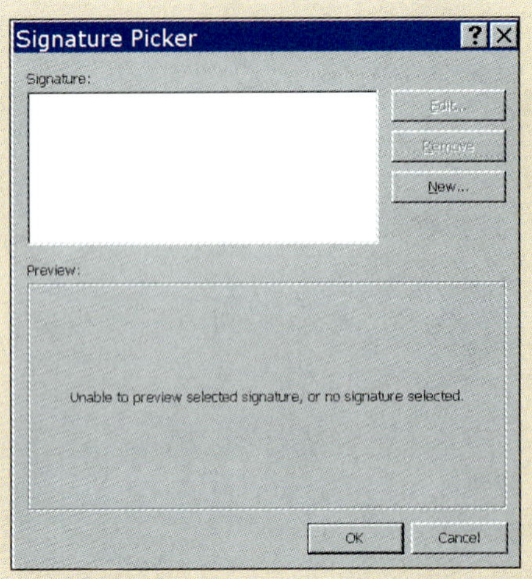

2 To create a new signature:
CLICK: New command button in the Signature Picker dialog box
TYPE: **My signature** in the *Enter a name...* text box

3 To proceed:
CLICK: Next command button
The Edit Signature dialog box should now appear and the insertion point is blinking in the *Signature text* area.

4 Create a signature that is similar to the one in Figure 3.23. However, at the same time, feel free to be creative.

Figure 3.23
Creating a signature

5 To proceed:
CLICK: Finish command button
CLICK: OK twice to return to the Outlook window

6 To view the new signature, let's start a new mail message.
CHOOSE: Actions, New Mail Message
Note how your signature was automatically inserted at the bottom of the message.

7 To close the message without saving:
CLICK: Close button (☒) of the message window

3.4.3 Sorting and Finding Mail

FEATURE
As your mail folders become filled with lots of messages, it can be difficult to locate desired messages. By default, messages are sorted in descending order of when they were received. For help in locating messages, you can easily change the sort order by clicking the column headings that display in the Information Viewer. You can also locate messages based on typed keywords.

METHOD
- To sort your message list:
  CLICK: the headings that appear at the top of the message list
- To find messages by searching header area text:
  CHOOSE: Tools, Find
  TYPE: **search text** in the *Look for* text box
  CLICK: Find Now command button
- To find messages by searching entire messages:
  CHOOSE: Tools, Advanced Find
  TYPE: **search text** in the *Search for the word(s)* text box
  SELECT: "subject field and message body" from the *In* drop-down list
  CLICK: Find Now command button

PRACTICE
In this lesson, you practice sorting your message list and finding messages based on typed text.

Setup: Ensure that you've completed the previous lessons in this module and that the contents of the Student Data Files folder are displaying.

1 The Student Data Files folder is currently in order by the Received column, with the most recent messages appearing first. To reverse the order of your message list:
CLICK: "Received" column heading

OUTLOOK

2. To sort your message list in order by the From column:
CLICK: "From" column heading

3. To re-sort your message list by the Received column:
CLICK: "Received" column heading
Your message list is now displaying in its original order.

4. Let's practice finding messages based on typed keywords.
CHOOSE: Tools, Find
Your screen should now appear similar to Figure 3.24. The Find pane now appears above the message list.

Figure 3.24
Finding items

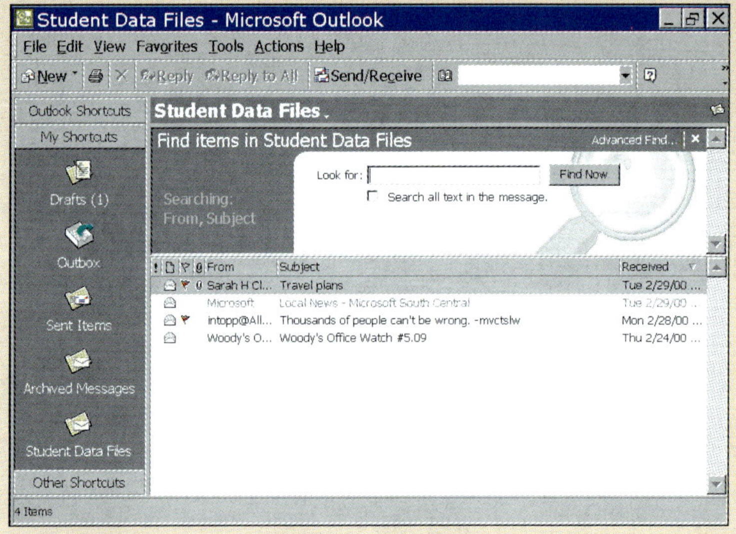

5. To find messages that contain the word "Microsoft" in the header area, do the following:
TYPE: **Microsoft** in the *Look for* text box
CLICK: Find Now command button
The message from Microsoft should be displaying in the list area. At this point, you can open the message by double-clicking it.

6. To perform a more advanced search where entire messages are searched for the word "people," do the following:
CHOOSE: Tools, Advanced Find
TYPE: **people** in the *Search for the word(s)* text box
SELECT: "subject field and message body" from the *In* drop-down list
CLICK: Find Now command button
Your screen should now appear similar to Figure 3.25.

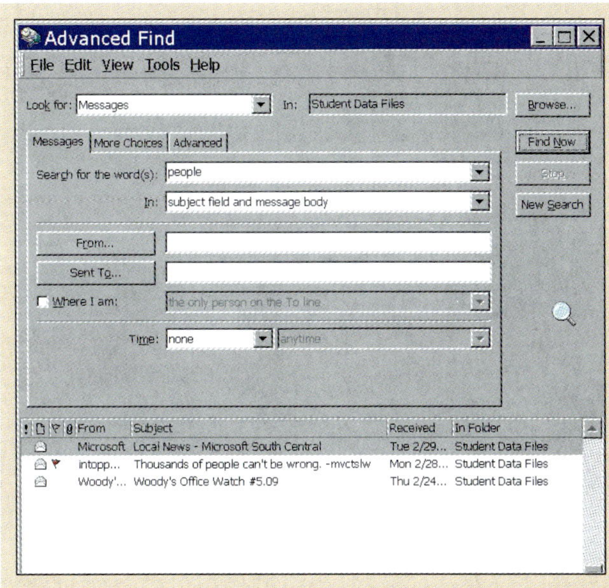

Figure 3.25
Advanced Find dialog box

7. To leave the Advanced Find dialog box:
   CLICK: its Close button (☒)

8. To remove the Find pane from the Information Viewer:
   CHOOSE: Tools, Find

9. Continue to the next lesson.

3.4.4 Archiving Mail

FEATURE

In Outlook, it's easy for messages to pile up in your Inbox folder. Over time, you will want to throw some messages away, while keeping others for referral later on. To help with this latter task, Outlook provides a command for saving older items to a storage, or *archive*, file.

METHOD

To create an archive file:

1. CHOOSE: File, Archive from the Menu bar
2. SELECT: a date from the *Archive items older than* drop-down list
3. CLICK: Browse command button and then navigate to a save location
4. CLICK: OK command button

To access items stored in an archived file:

1. SELECT: the folder you originally archived messages from
2. CHOOSE: File, Import and Export
3. SELECT: "Import from another program or file" from the list box
4. CLICK: Next command button
5. SELECT: "Personal Folder File (.pst)" from the list box
6. CLICK: Next command button
7. CLICK: Browse command button and then navigate to where your archive file is stored
8. CLICK: Next command button
9. CLICK: Finish command button

PRACTICE

In this lesson, you archive all the files stored in the Student Data Files folder.

Setup: Ensure that you've completed the previous lessons in this module and that the contents of the Student Data Files folder are displaying.

1 CHOOSE: File, Archive
The Archive dialog box should now appear (Figure 3.26).

Figure 3.26
Archive dialog box

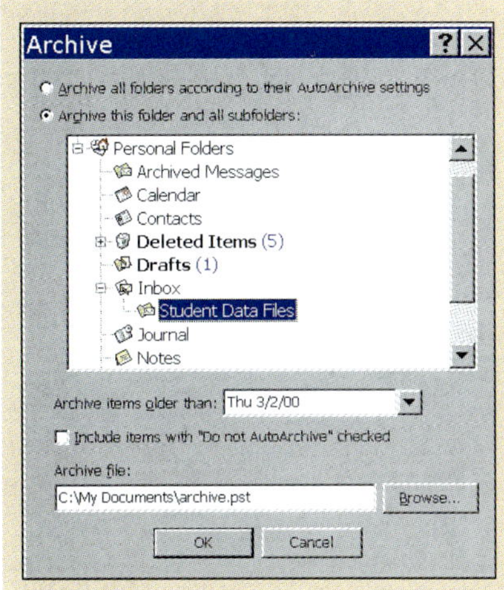

2 To archive items that were sent before today's date:
CLICK: *Archive items older than* drop-down arrow
CLICK: Today command button

3 To store the archive file in your personal storage location:
CLICK: Browse command button

4 Navigate to your personal storage location.

5 To proceed:
CLICK: OK command button

6 If you look in the *Archive file* text box, you'll see that your archive file will be named "archive.pst."
CLICK: OK command button to continue
The message "Archiving" should be displaying in the bottom-right corner of the Information Viewer. At the conclusion of the archive procedure, no files should be displaying in the Student Data Files folder. They've all been moved to a file named "archive.pst" stored in your personal storage location.

7 Not only is it important to know how to archive older files, but it's also important to know how to get them back. The following steps lead you through retrieving your archived items back into your Student Data Files folder. Before continuing, ensure that the Student Data Files folder is open.

8 To import the archived items back into the Student Data Files folder:
CHOOSE: File, Import and Export
The Import and Export wizard is launched.

9 SELECT: "Import from another program or file" from the list box
CLICK: Next command button

10 SELECT: "Personal Folder File (.pst)" from the list box
CLICK: Next command button

11 CLICK: Browse command button

12 Navigate to your personal storage location where the "archive.pst" file is stored.

13 CLICK: Next command button
CLICK: Finish command button
The archived items should reappear in your Student Data Files folder.

In Addition
Filtering Mail

The good news is that it's very cheap to use e-mail as a communication medium. The bad news is that it's very cheap to use e-mail as a communication medium. That is, anybody can send you e-mail, which leads to all sorts of junk finding its way into your Inbox. Fortunately, Outlook can filter out unwanted mail and send it straight to the trash bin. To filter out unwanted mail, Outlook searches incoming mail for off-color and solicitous phrases and automatically changes the color of suspect messages or moves them to the Deleted Items folder or to another folder of your choice. The list of terms that Outlook uses to filter your messages is stored in a file named Filters.txt. To filter messages, open your Inbox folder (or another mail folder) and then choose Tools, Organize. Then, click the Junk E-Mail link and click the Turn on command buttons. (*Note:* You can also download third-party filters from the Web and add them to Outlook. For more information on this topic, visit Outlook's Web site at www.microsoft.com/outlook.)

3.4 Self Check In Outlook, what is a signature?

3.5 Integrating Outlook Mail with Other Tools and Applications

Do you know that from within Outlook you can create Office documents for delivery via e-mail? In this module, we explore integrating Outlook mail with Microsoft Office 2000 and sharing information between Outlook mail and your contact list.

3.5.1 Integrating Mail with Office 2000

FEATURE

Without ever leaving Outlook, you can create new Office documents from scratch, thus avoiding the inconvenience of switching between applications and inserting message attachments. When you create an Office 2000 document from within Outlook, the Menu bar and toolbars of your source application appear in the message window.

METHOD

1. CHOOSE: File, New, Office Document
2. DOUBLE-CLICK: the type of document you want to create
3. SELECT: an option button in the Microsoft Outlook dialog box
4. CLICK: OK command button

PRACTICE

You will now create a new Word document and send it to a friend.

Setup: Ensure that Outlook is loaded and that you prepared the student data files in Module 3.1.

1 Open the Student Data Files folder.

2 To create a new Microsoft Word 2000 document without leaving Outlook:
CHOOSE: File, New, Office Document
The New Office Document dialog box should now appear.

3 DOUBLE-CLICK: the Microsoft Word Document icon
The dialog box shown below should now display. The *Post the document in this folder* option button creates the document and saves it in the current folder. The *Send the document to someone* option button creates the document and sends it to someone else via e-mail.

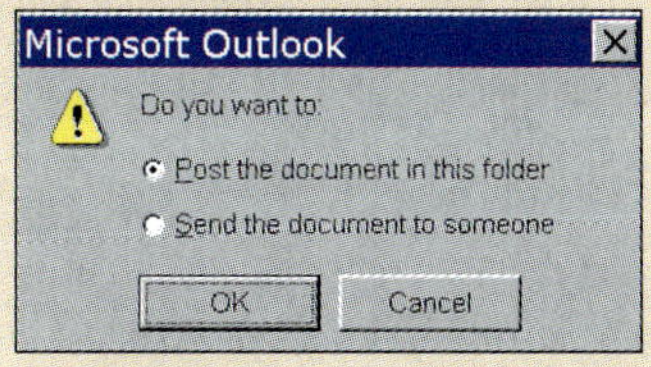

4. Let's select the second option button:
SELECT: *Send the document to someone* option button
CLICK: OK command button
Your screen should now appear similar to Figure 3.27. Note the two tabs in the document window. The *Message* tab, which is currently displaying in Figure 3.27, is used for addressing your message. The *Document* tab is used for composing your message.

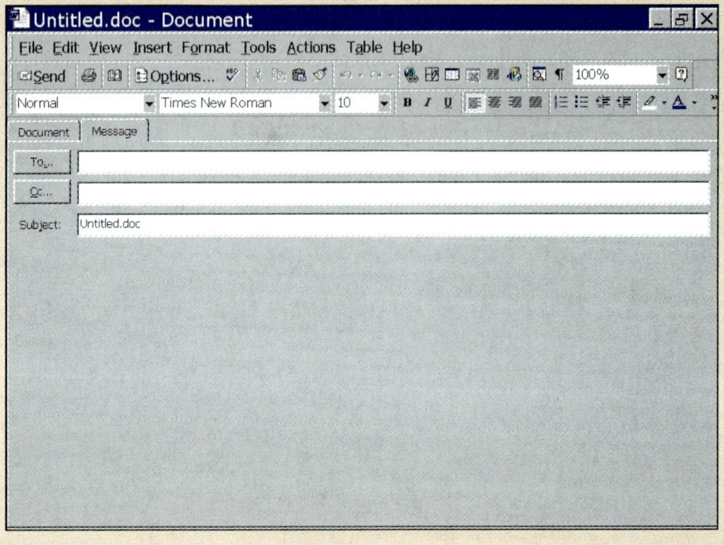

Figure 3.27
Addressing a Word document

5. The insertion point is blinking in the *To* text box.
TYPE: ***a friend's e-mail address***

6. SELECT: the text in the *Subject* text box
TYPE: ***a subject of your choice***

7. To compose your message:
CLICK: *Document* tab
Your screen should now appear similar to Figure 3.28. Note that you have access to all of Word's menu and toolbar options.

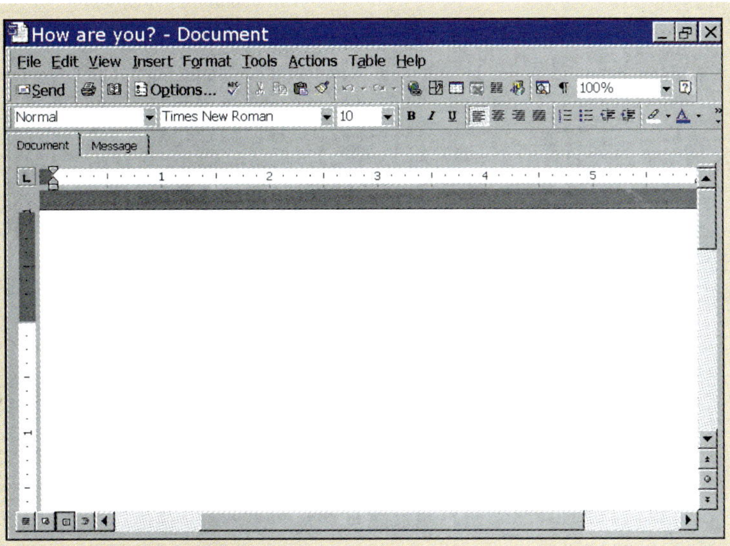

Figure 3.28
Composing a Word document

8 TYPE: a message of your choice

9 To send the message:
CLICK: Send button on the Standard toolbar
The message was moved to your Outbox folder. When your recipient receives and then opens the message, the *Document* tab will automatically display.

10 Continue to the next lesson.

3.5.2 Integrating Mail with Your Contact List

FEATURE
As you probably already know, Outlook's tools are designed to work together. In Chapter 2, for example, you learned how to create task items using the Calendar tool. In this lesson, you send e-mail to an existing contact, forward contact information in an e-mail message, and create contact items from received mail messages.

METHOD

To send e-mail to an existing contact:

1. RIGHT-CLICK: a contact item
2. CHOOSE: New Message to Contact from the right-click menu

To send contact information via e-mail:

1. RIGHT-CLICK: a contact item
2. CHOOSE: Forward as vCard from the right-click menu

To add e-mail addresses to your contact list:

1. Open an existing mail message.
2. RIGHT-CLICK: the e-mail address in the *From* or *To* field
3. CHOOSE: Add to Contacts from the right-click menu

PRACTICE

In this lesson, you practice integrating Outlook mail with your contact list.

Setup: Ensure that you've completed the previous lesson and that the contents of your Student Data Files folder are displaying.

1 Let's send an e-mail message to someone in your contact list. Locate a contact item in your contact list that includes an e-mail address.

2 CLICK: Contacts icon ( ) in the Outlook Bar
RIGHT-CLICK: the contact item you located in step 1
CHOOSE: New Message to Contact option from the right-click menu
Note that the message window opened and your contact's e-mail address was automatically inserted in the *To* text box. To proceed, you would simply fill in the *Subject* field and proceed with composing the message.

3 Close the message window without saving.

4 To forward someone's contact information to somebody else, do the following:
RIGHT-CLICK: an existing contact item
CHOOSE: Forward as vCard from the right-click menu
Your screen should now appear similar, but not identical, to Figure 3.29. When your recipient receives this message, he or she must simply double-click the contact attachment to view its contents.

Figure 3.29
Forwarding contact information

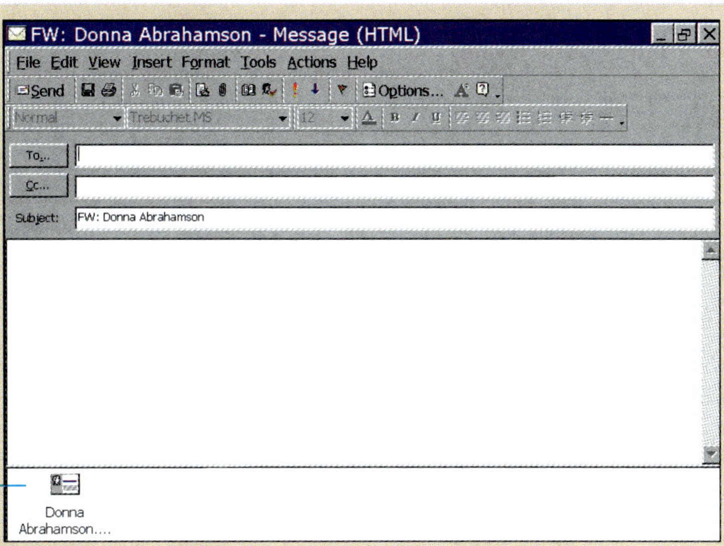

5 Close the window without saving.

6 Finally, to add an e-mail address to your contact database, do the following:
CLICK: Student Data Files icon ( ) in the Outlook Bar
DOUBLE-CLICK: the Microsoft message in the Information Viewer

7 To add Microsoft's address to your contact database:
RIGHT-CLICK: Microsoft's address in the *From* field
CHOOSE: Add to Contacts from the right-click menu
The Contact window should have opened. Note that Microsoft's information was automatically inserted in the dialog box.

8 Close the contact window without saving.

9 Close the message window.

3.5 Self Check What is the procedure for creating an Excel worksheet from within Outlook?

OUTLOOK

3.6 Chapter Review

Using Outlook's mail features, it's easy to stay in touch with friends and coworkers. When addressing a new message, you can either type your recipient's e-mail address or copy it from your contact list. After typing in a subject for your message, you will want to compose your message and, optionally, format your message, insert an attachment, or assign a message flag. When you click the Send button, your message is moved to your Outbox folder for later delivery. Received messages display in your Inbox folder. Using Outlook, you can easily reply to messages, and forward, print, and find messages.

3.6.1 Command Summary

Many of the commands and procedures appearing in this chapter are summarized in the following table.

Skill Set	To Perform This Task . . .	Do the Following . . .
Use Outlook Mail	Addressing mail by entering text	In the message window: CLICK: in the *To* or *Cc* text box TYPE: **an e-mail address**
	Addressing mail using your contact list	In the message window: CLICK: To command button, or CLICK: Cc command button
	Sending mail	CLICK: Send button in the message window CLICK: Send/Receive button
	Composing mail	In the message window: CLICK: in the large text area TYPE: **your message**
	Inserting an attachment	CLICK: Insert File button (📎), or CHOOSE: Insert, File
	Flagging messages	In the message window: CLICK: Flag for Follow Up button (🚩)

Continued

Skill Set	To Perform This Task . . .	Do the Following . . .
Use Outlook Mail *Continued*	Assigning an importance level	In the message window: CLICK: Importance: High button ( ), or CLICK: Importance: Low button ( )
	Reading mail	DOUBLE-CLICK: a message
	Navigating within mail	In the message window: CLICK: Previous Item ( ), or CLICK: Next Item ( ) button
	Printing mail	CHOOSE: File, Print, or CLICK: Print button ( )
	Configuring basic print options	CHOOSE: File, Print CLICK: Page Setup command button
	Replying to messages	CLICK: Reply button ( )
	Forwarding messages	CLICK: Forward button ( )
	Opening attached files	DOUBLE-CLICK: the attachment icon CHOOSE: *Open it* option button
	Saving attached files	RIGHT-CLICK: the attachment icon CHOOSE: Save As
	Changing fonts for new messages	CHOOSE: Tools, Options CLICK: *Mail Format* tab CLICK: Fonts command button
	Applying a mail template	CHOOSE: Tools, Options CLICK: *Mail Format* tab CLICK: Stationery Picker command button
	Creating a signature	CHOOSE: Tools, Options CLICK: *Mail Format* tab CLICK: Signature Picker command button
	Finding mail	CHOOSE: Tools, Find, or CHOOSE: Tools, Advanced Find

Continued

OUTLOOK

Skill Set	To Perform This Task . . .	Do the Following . . .
Use Outlook 2000 to Manage Messages	Creating a message folder	CHOOSE: File, Folder, New
	Sorting mail	CLICK: headings that appear at the top of the message list
	Archiving mail	CHOOSE: File, Archive
	Filtering mail	CHOOSE: Tools, Organize CLICK: Junk E-Mail link
Use Contacts	Sending contact information via e-mail	RIGHT-CLICK: a contact item CHOOSE: Forward as vCard
Integrate Office Applications with Outlook 2000	Integrating mail with Office 2000	CHOOSE: File, New, Office Document

3.7 Review Questions

3.7.1 Short Answer

1. How do you sort message items in Outlook?
2. With your contact list displaying, what is the procedure for sending an e-mail message to one of your contacts?
3. In Outlook, why might you want to create a new mail folder?
4. What is the procedure for addressing a message using addresses stored in your contact list?
5. What is a message flag?
6. What is the difference between replying to a message and forwarding a message?
7. What is the purpose for applying a mail template to new messages?
8. What happens when you *archive* older messages?
9. Using Outlook, what is the procedure for creating a new Office document from scratch?
10. What is the procedure for forwarding contact information to someone else?

3.7.2 True/False

1. ____ E-mail addresses consist of a user name, followed by @, followed by a domain name.

2. ____ Inbox provides the perfect tool for organizing appointments.
3. ____ In Outlook, it's possible to add an e-mail address from a received message to your contact list.
4. ____ In Outlook, it's possible to filter out messages that contain adult content.
5. ____ Archive files can't be opened using Outlook; you must use a separate archive application.
6. ____ When composing an e-mail message, you must supply an e-mail address in the *To* field.
7. ____ To compose a message in Outlook, simply click in the large text area in the message window and begin typing.
8. ____ In Outlook, Web addresses are automatically formatted as hyperlinks.
9. ____ Before you can compose an e-mail message, you must create a contact list using the Contacts tool.
10. ____ Using the Formatting toolbar, you can format your messages with special fonts and sizes and with varied paragraph formatting affecting alignment and indentation.

3.7.3 Multiple Choice

1. Which of the following is a valid e-mail address?
   a. mary@friend.com
   b. www.friend.com
   c. friend.com
   d. all of the above

2. If your recipient's e-mail program does not support message formatting, the received message will appear __________.
   a. as plain text
   b. in bold letters
   c. as an attached icon
   d. none of the above

3. By default, when you click the Send button in the message window, your message is __________.
   a. saved to your Inbox folder
   b. saved to your Outbox folder
   c. saved to your Sent Items folder
   d. sent to the message recipient

4. In an e-mail message, an inserted graphics file appears as a(n):
   a. flag
   b. folder
   c. icon
   d. none of the above

5. When you receive a message attachment, you open it by:
   a. clicking it once
   b. double-clicking
   c. right-clicking
   d. none of the above

6. How does Outlook notify you that you've received messages?
   a. by a mail icon () on the taskbar
   b. by displaying number in parentheses next to the Inbox icon in the Outlook bar
   c. by formatting the titles of new messages in bold letters for display in the Information Viewer
   d. all of the above

7. Which of the following symbols indicates that a message has been flagged?
   a.
   b. 
   c. 
   d. 

8. To search the contents of entire messages, you must use the __________________.
   a. Sort dialog box
   b. Find dialog box
   c. Advanced Find dialog box
   d. none of the above

9. Which of the following techniques enables you to remove messages from your Inbox folder without deleting them?
   a. archiving
   b. creating a folder
   c. attaching files
   d. all of the above

10. Using Outlook's Formatting toolbar, you can:
    a. format your messages with special fonts and sizes
    b. apply varied paragraph formatting
    c. change alignment and indentation
    d. all of the above

3.8 Hands-On Projects

3.8.1 Creative Design Picture Framing: Sending an Announcement Letter

In this exercise, you practice addressing and composing a short message.

1. To begin a new e-mail message, do the following:
   CLICK: Inbox icon ( ) in the Outlook Bar
   CLICK: New Mail Message button (New) on the Standard toolbar
2. To address the message:
   TYPE: **customer@practice.com** in the *To* text box
   CLICK: in the *Subject* text box
   TYPE: **Creative Design Picture Framing!**
3. To compose your message:
   CLICK: in the large text area
   TYPE: **Dear prospective customer,**
   PRESS: ENTER twice
   TYPE: **We are a complete framing source. Everything you need to frame it yourself: wood and metal frames, matboard, equipment, and supplies. Compare our prices and quality of products. Gallery-quality wood frames at do-it-yourself prices. We do not have a minimum order and we provide free hardware with all orders. Most orders shipped within 3 to 4 days. Visit our Web site at www.creativedesign.com!!**
   PRESS: ENTER twice
   TYPE: **Sincerely,**
   PRESS: ENTER twice
   TYPE: ***your name***
   PRESS: ENTER once
   TYPE: **President**

4. To move the message to your Outbox for later delivery:
   CLICK: Send button on the Standard toolbar

OUTLOOK

5. Let's edit the letter that's located in your Outbox.
   CLICK: My Shortcuts group button on the Outlook Bar
   CLICK: Outbox icon ( )
   DOUBLE-CLICK: the "Creative Design Picture Framing!" message
6. To assign a high importance level to this message:
   CLICK: Importance: High button ( ) on the Standard toolbar
7. To print a copy of this message:
   CLICK: Print button ( ) on the Standard toolbar
8. To again move the message to your Outbox for later delivery:
   CLICK: Send button on the Standard toolbar
9. As a final step, let's delete the message from your Outbox folder:
   CLICK: the message
   CLICK: Delete button ( ) on the Standard toolbar

3.8.2 Summit Career College: Replying to a Message

This exercise practices replying to a message, inserting a message flag, and assigning an importance level.

1. Employed in the admissions office at Summit Career College, you've just received a message and you need to reply to it.
   SELECT: "Fall Schedule" message in your Student Data Files folder
   CLICK: Reply button ( )
2. Normally, when replying to a message, the sender's e-mail address will appear in the *To* field. We've left this field blank on purpose.
   TYPE: **your e-mail address** in the *To* text box
3. To type in a response:
   CLICK: above the existing message text
   TYPE: **Hi Ricardo,**
   PRESS: ENTER
   TYPE: **You'll find the schedule information you're looking for at www.summitcollege.com/schedules.**
   PRESS: ENTER
   TYPE: **Good luck!**
4. Now, let's apply a message flag to the message.
   CLICK: Flag for Follow Up button ( )
   SELECT: "For Your Information" from the *Flag to* drop-down list
   CLICK: OK command button
5. To move this folder to your Outbox folder:
   CLICK: Send button on the Standard toolbar
6. To print a copy of this message:
   CLICK: Print button ( ) on the Standard toolbar

7. To again move the message to your Outbox folder:
   CLICK: Send button on the Standard toolbar
8. To deliver the message over the Internet:
   CLICK: Send/Receive button

3.8.3 Rapunzel's Hair Design: E-Mailing a Contact

In this exercise, you add a contact to your contact list, compose an e-mail message to the contact, insert a message attachment, and assign an importance level.

1. Add the following contact information to your contact list:
   Gloria Reynolds
   2231 Johnson Drive
   Three Rivers, California 93271
   E-mail: **greynolds@pretend.com**
2. Print out your contact listing.
3. Send an e-mail message to your contact. Include **"About Coloring Your Hair"** in the *Subject* text box and the following text in the message area: **I've attached the document I talked to you about. See you in 6 weeks!**
4. Attach the data file named "Coloring Your Hair" to the current message. This file is located in your personal storage location.
5. Assign a low importance level to the message.
6. Preview and then print the message.
7. Send the message to your Outbox folder.
8. Delete the message from your Outbox folder.

3.8.4 Armstrong Equipment Rental: Managing a Mail Folder

In this exercise, you practice sorting, finding, and archiving messages in the Student Data Files folder.

1. Display the list of messages stored in your Student Data Files folder. You created this folder in Module 3.1.
2. Find a message that contains the phrase "retire this year" in the body of the message.
3. Print out the message you located in step 2.
4. Sort the messages in the Student Data Files folder in ascending order by the *Subject* field.
5. Print your message list using the Table Style.
6. Archive the contents of the Student Data Files folder to your personal storage location.
7. Restore the messages you archived in step 6 to their original folder.

OUTLOOK

3.8.5 On Your Own: Creating a Signature

Create a signature file that contains the text you want to display at the end of all your outgoing messages. Then, start a new message describing the steps you took to create your signature. (*Note:* If your signature text is displaying too closely to your typed text, edit your signature to include one or more blank lines.) Print your message and then close the message window without saving.

3.8.6 On Your Own: Selecting a Format for New Messages

Use the *Mail Format* tab of the Options dialog box to define a look for new mail messages. Select an existing mail template to apply to new messages and then edit the mail template to include your personal preferences. (*Hint:* To edit a mail template, choose Tools, Options and click the Stationery Picker command button. Then after selecting a template in the list box, click the Edit command button.) Create a new message describing the changes you made to the mail template and then print it out. Close the message window without saving.

3.9 Case Problems: Sleepy Hollow Community Center

Now that Mary has successfully performed all the steps in this chapter, she is ready to begin using Outlook's mail features to respond to donor inquiries. For the past several weeks, she has been asking people for their e-mail addresses, explaining to them that e-mail will help her to perform her job more efficiently.

In the following case problems, assume the role of Mary and perform the same steps that she identifies. You may want to re-read the chapter opening before proceeding.

1. Mary has decided to draft a newsletter for existing donors describing plans for the new Sleepy Hollow Community Center. She's decided to use Word 2000 to create the body of the letter. She begins by displaying the contents of the Student Data Files folder (created in Module 3.1). Next, she chooses File, New, Office Document and then double-clicks the Microsoft Word document icon. In the dialog box that displays, she selects the *Post the document in this folder* option button.

In the Word window, Mary types the following: **The Center design is the result of a detailed community needs analysis, community surveys, and public hearings and features 37,000 square feet in two two-story buildings joined by covered walkways and landscaping.** Interrupted by the ring of a phone, Mary answers the phone and then clicks the Post button (Post) on the Standard toolbar.

2. Mary has finished the letter that she began in the previous exercise and has copied it into her personal storage location. Start a new message and include your e-mail address in the *To* text box and the text **Sleepy Hollow Community Center Information** in the *Subject* text box. Next, flag the message with the text "For Your Information." In the message area, type ***Recipient's name,*** **Here's the information I promised you. Let me know if you have further questions. Sincerely, Mary.** Finally, attach the file named "Community Center News" (stored in your personal storage location) to the message. Before sending the letter, open the message attachment and then print a copy. Finally, send the message.

3. Mary has decided to forward her contact information to existing donors in case they have misplaced it. She creates a new contact and adds the following information to her contact database:

   Mary Rexroat
   Campaign Director
   Sleepy Hollow Community Center
   140 Rogers Way
   Sleepy Hollow, IL 60541
   221-111-1010
   mrexroat@shcc.com

   Before forwarding her contact information to existing donors, she forwards it to herself. Upon receiving the message, she opens the "vCard" attachment and prints its contents.

4. Mary decides to create a signature for all of her outgoing messages. She includes the following information in the signature file:

   Sleepy Hollow Community Center
   Let's make it a reality!
   Mary Rexroat, Campaign Director
   (Tel) 221-111-1010

   After creating the signature, Mary starts a new message and then prints a copy of the message window. She then closes the message window without saving. (*Note:* Before continuing, return your signature to its original state.)

NOTES

NOTES

Answers to Self Check Questions

1.1 Self Check Why is it important to know how to change the current view in Outlook? In selecting a view for your data, you display it in a format suited to your needs. Since your needs might not be the same as someone else's, Microsoft gives you several views to choose from.

1.2 Self Check By default, how is your contact list sorted into order? Unless you specify otherwise, your contact list is sorted in order by the File As field.

1.3 Self Check What is the Notes tool used for? The Notes tool can be used to create electronic sticky notes for reminding you of details that might otherwise get past you.

1.4 Self Check What is context-sensitive help? Context-sensitive help refers to a software program's ability to retrieve and present helpful information reflecting your current position in the program.

2.1 Self Check What is the procedure for saving your calendar to HTML for publishing on a Web server? Choose File, Save as Web Page from the Menu bar.

2.2 Self Check What features of the Tasks tool do you find the most useful? *Answers will vary.* The Tasks tool provides a convenient means for tracking tasks that you still need to perform or that are currently under way. Task items can be programmed to remind you when a task should be performed, and you can create tasks that must be completed on a recurring basis.

2.3 Self Check In Outlook, what are categories used for? Categories are used for sorting, finding, and grouping Outlook items.

2.4 Self Check What procedure would you use to remove a button from the Standard toolbar? To remove a button from the Standard toolbar, simply drag it away from the toolbar.

3.1 Self Check What two types of software do you need before you can send and receive e-mail? First, you need software such as Outlook for composing and managing e-mail messages. Second, you need software for transporting your e-mail to and from other people over the Internet.

3.2 Self Check When might you want to add a flag to a message? When you want to provide recipients with additional information and reminders relating to your message. For example, you can remind recipients to respond to your message by a certain date.

3.3 Self Check What does it mean to reply to a message? When you reply to a message, you send a message back to the sender of the original message. In addition to your comments, a message reply includes a copy of the original message.

3.4 Self Check In Outlook, what is a signature? A signature is text that appears on the bottom of all your outgoing messages.

3.5 Self Check What is the procedure for creating an Excel worksheet from within Outlook? Choose File, New, Office Document and then double-click the Microsoft Excel Worksheet icon.

Glossary

Calendar A Microsoft Outlook tool for keeping track of your schedule.

Contacts A Microsoft Outlook tool for maintaining an address database.

context-sensitive help Help information that relates to your current position in a program.

HTML An acronym for Hypertext Markup Language, which is the standardized markup language used in creating documents for display on the World Wide Web.

Inbox A Microsoft Outlook tool for managing your e-mail.

Journal A Microsoft Outlook tool for keeping track of the tasks you perform on a single timeline.

Microsoft Exchange Server Software stored on computer networks to enable collaboration and information sharing.

Microsoft Outlook 2000 A personal information manager for keeping track of everyday information such as dates, addresses, reminder notes, and e-mail messages.

Notes A Microsoft Outlook tool for posting "sticky" notes within Outlook or on the Windows desktop.

Office Clipboard A program in Office 2000 that allows you to copy and move information within or among Office 2000 applications. Unlike the Windows Clipboard, the Office Clipboard can store up to 12 items and then paste them all at once.

Outlook Today A Microsoft Outlook folder that provides an overview of activities relating to the current day.

Tasks A Microsoft Outlook tool for tracking tasks that need to be performed.

Windows Clipboard A program in Windows that allows you to copy and move information within an application or among applications. The Windows Clipboard temporarily stores the information in memory before you paste the data in a new location.

Appendix: Microsoft Windows Quick Reference

Using the Mouse and Keyboard

Microsoft Windows provides a graphical environment for working in your application, such as Microsoft Word, Excel, Access, or PowerPoint. As you work with Windows applications, you will find that there are often three different ways to perform the same command. The most common methods for performing commands include:

• Menu	Choose a command from the Menu bar or from a right-click menu.
• Mouse	Position the mouse pointer over a toolbar button and then click once.
• Keyboard	Press a keyboard shortcut (usually CTRL + ***letter***).

Although you may use a Windows application with only a keyboard, much of a program's basic design relies on using a mouse. Regardless of whether your mouse has two or three buttons, you will use the left or primary mouse button for selecting screen objects and menu commands and the right or secondary mouse button for displaying right-click menus.

The most common mouse actions include:

• Point	Slide the mouse on your desk to position the tip of the mouse pointer over the desired object on the screen.
• Click	Press down and release the left mouse button quickly. Clicking is used to select a screen object, activate a toolbar command, and choose menu commands.
• Right-Click	Press down and release the right mouse button. Right-clicking the mouse pointer on a screen object displays a context-sensitive menu.
• Double-Click	Press down and release the mouse button twice in rapid succession. Double-clicking is used to select screen objects or to activate an embedded object for editing.
• Drag	Press down and hold the mouse button as you move the mouse pointer across the screen. When the mouse pointer reaches the desired location, release the mouse button. Dragging is used to select a group of screen objects and to copy or move data.

You may notice that the mouse pointer changes shape as you move it over different parts of the screen. Each mouse pointer shape has its own purpose and may provide you with important information. There are four primary mouse shapes that appear in Windows applications:

	arrow	Used to choose menu commands and click toolbar buttons.
	hourglass	Informs you that the application is occupied and requests that you wait.
	I-beam	Used to set the position of the insertion point and to modify and edit text.
	hand	Used to select hyperlinks in the Windows-based Help systems, in Microsoft Office documents, and on the Web.

Aside from being the primary input device for entering information, the keyboard offers shortcut methods for performing some common commands and procedures.

Starting Windows

Because Windows is an operating system, it is loaded into the computer's memory when you first turn on the computer. To start Windows, you must do the following:

1. Turn on the power switches to the computer and monitor. After a few seconds, the Windows desktop will appear. (*Note:* If you are attached to a network, a dialog box may appear asking you to enter your User name and Password. Enter this information now or ask your instructor for further instructions.)
2. A Welcome dialog box may appear providing information about the operating system's major features. If the Welcome dialog box appears on your screen:
   CLICK: Close button (×) in the top right-hand corner of the Welcome window
3. If additional windows appear open on your desktop:
   CLICK: Close button (×) in the top right-hand corner of each window

Parts of a Dialog Box

A dialog box is a common mechanism in Windows applications for collecting information before processing a command. In a dialog box, you indicate the options you want to use and then click the OK button when you're finished. Dialog boxes are also used to display messages or to ask for the confirmation of commands. The following shows an example of the Print dialog box, which is similar across Windows applications.

Print dialog box

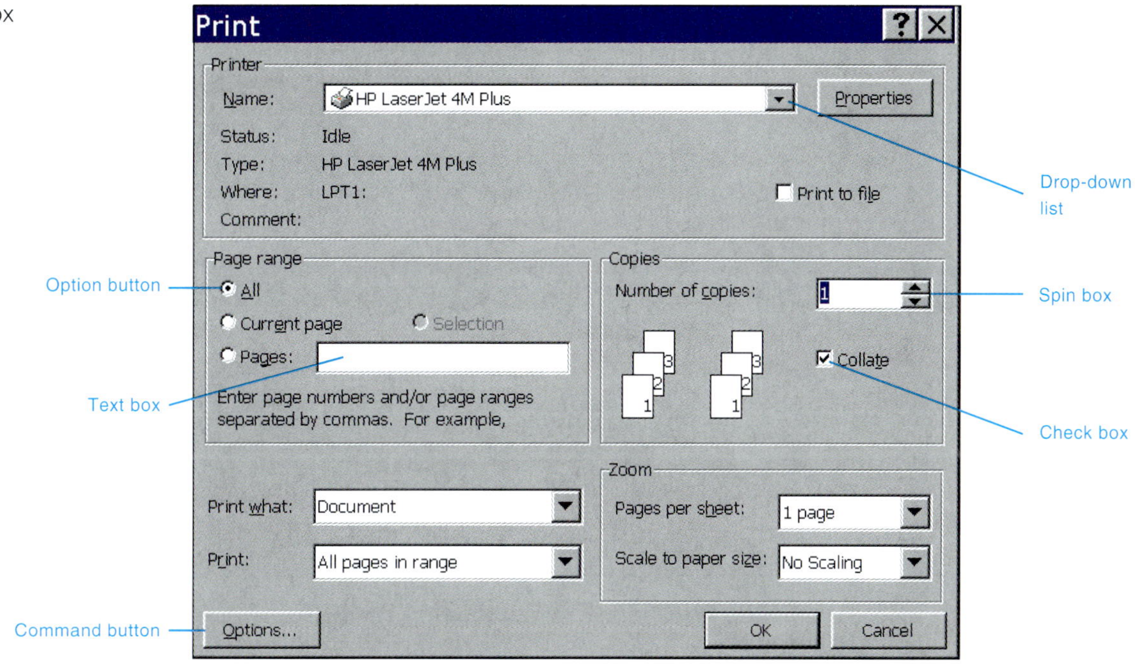

A dialog box uses several types of controls or components for collecting information. We describe the most common components in the following table.

Dialog box components

Name	*Example*	*Action*
Check box		Click an option to turn it on or off. The option is turned on when a "✔" appears in the box.
Command button	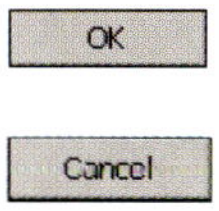	Click a command button to execute an action. Click OK to acccpt your selections or click Cancel to exit the dialog box.

Continued

Name	*Example*	*Action*
Drop-down list box		Make a choice from the list that appears when you click the down arrow next to the box; only the selected choice is visible.
List box		Make a choice from the scrollable list; several choices, if not all, are always visible.
Option button		Select an option from a group of related options.
Slide box	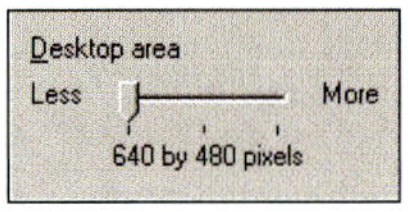	Drag the slider bar to make a selection, like using a radio's volume control.
Spin box		Click the up and down arrows to the right of the box until the number you want appears.
Tab		Click a named tab at the top of the window to access other pages of options in the dialog box.
Text box		Click inside the text box and then type the desired information.

Most dialog boxes provide a question mark icon (?) near the right side of the Title bar. If you have a question about an item in the dialog box, click the question mark and then click the item to display a pop-up Help window. To remove the Help window, click on it once.

Getting Help

Windows applications, such as Microsoft Office 2000 applications, provide a comprehensive library of online documentation. This section describes these help features and how to find more detailed information.

Obtaining Context-Sensitive Help

In Windows applications, you can often retrieve context-sensitive help for menu options, toolbar buttons, and dialog box items. *Context-sensitive help* refers to a program's ability to present helpful information reflecting your current position in the program. The help information is presented concisely in a small pop-up window that you can remove with the click of the mouse. This type of help lets you access information quickly and then continue working without interruption. The following table describes some methods for accessing context-sensitive help while working in Windows applications.

Displaying context-sensitive Help information

To display...	*Do this...*
A description of a dialog box item	Click the question mark button ([?]) in a dialog box's Title bar and then click an item in the dialog box. Alternatively, you can often right-click a dialog box item and then choose the What's This? command from the shortcut menu.
A description of a menu command	Choose the Help, What's This? command from the menu and then choose a command using the question mark mouse pointer. Rather than executing the command, a helpful description of the command appears in a pop-up window.
A description of a toolbar button	Point to a toolbar button to display a pop-up label called a ToolTip.

Getting Help in Office 2000

Getting Help from the Office Assistant

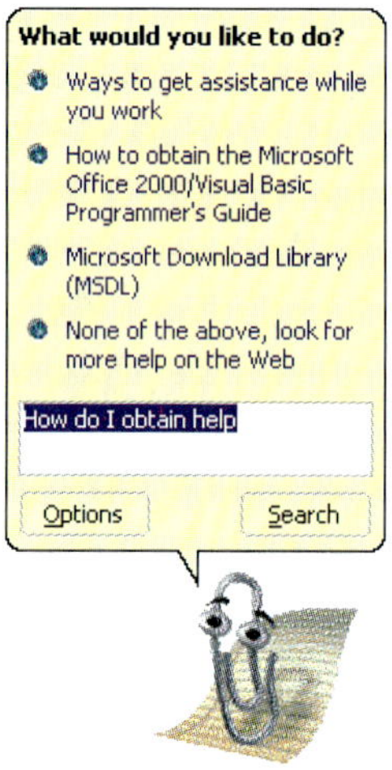

In Office 2000 applications, the Office Assistant is your personal computer guru and is available by default when your application is first installed. When you need to perform a task that you're unsure of, simply click the Assistant character and then type a phrase such as "How do I obtain help" in the Assistant balloon. The Assistant analyzes your request and provides a resource list of suggested topics, as shown to the right. Simply click a topic to obtain additional information.

The Assistant also watches your keystrokes and mouse clicks as you work and offers suggestions and shortcuts to make you more productive and efficient. If you find the Office Assistant to be distracting, you can turn it off by choosing "Hide the Office Assistant" from the Help menu. To redisplay it, simply choose "Microsoft *Application* Help" or "Show the Office Assistant" from the Help menu.

Getting Help from the Help Window

You may prefer to obtain a complete topical listing of your application's Help system. To do this, you must first disable the Office Assistant by clicking the Options button in the Assistant balloon, clearing the *Use the Office Assistant* check box, and then pressing ENTER. Once the Office Assistant is disabled, simply choose "Microsoft *Application* Help" from the Help menu to display the Help window. If the *Contents*, *Answer Wizard*, and *Index* tabs don't appear, click Show ( ) in the window's toolbar.

The Help window, shown next, provides three different tools, each on its own tab, to help you find the information you need quickly and easily. You can read the Help information you find on-screen or print it out for later reference by clicking the Print button ( ) in the window's toolbar. To close the Help window, click its Close button ( ).

Example Help window

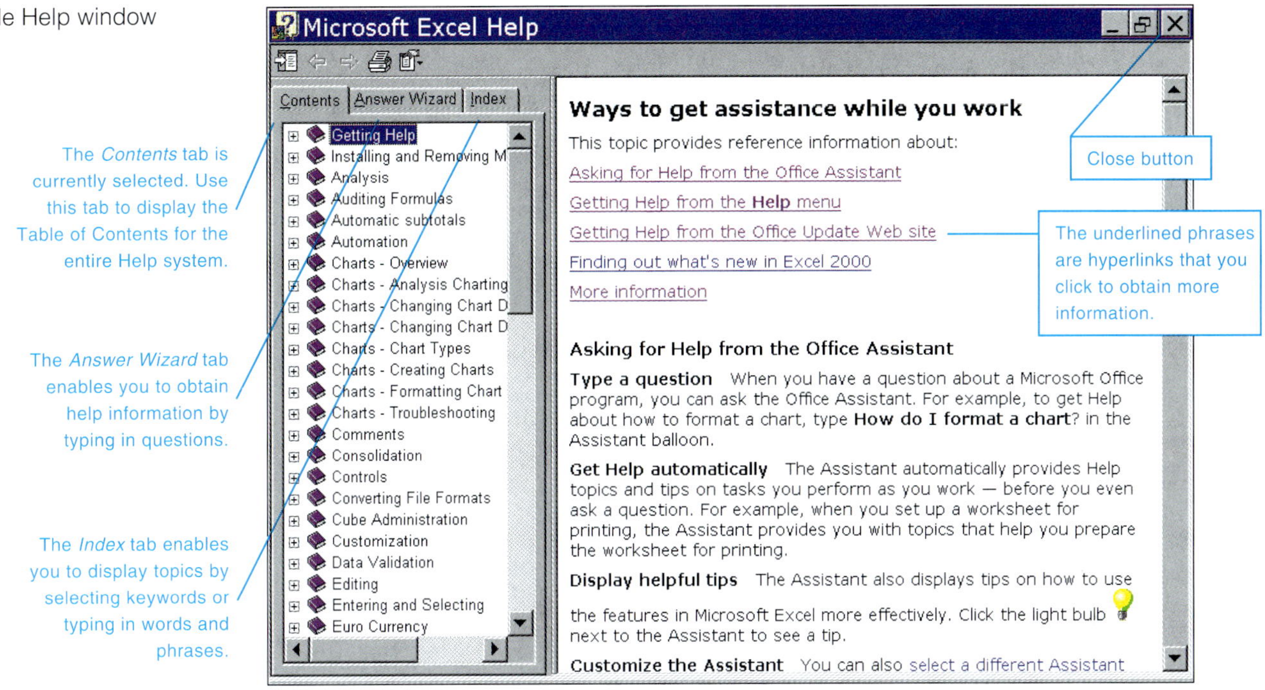

Getting Help from the Office Update Web Site

Microsoft's Office Update Web site provides additional technical support and product enhancements. You can access this site from any Office application by choosing "Office on the Web" from the Help menu.

Index

Microsoft Outlook 2000 Level 1 MOUS Objectives
Total Objectives: 59

MOUS Standardized Performance	Activity	Performance Based	Advantage Series Chapter/Module
OL2000.1	**Use Outlook 2000 Mail to communicate with others inside and outside your company**	**Yes**	0
OL2000.1.1	Read mail	**Yes**	3.3.1
OL2000.1.2	Send mail	**Yes**	3.2.2
OL2000.1.3	Compose mail by entering text	**Yes**	3.2.1
OL2000.1.4	Print mail	**Yes**	3.3.2
OL2000.1.5	Address mail by entering text	**Yes**	3.2.1
OL2000.1.6	Use mail features (forward, reply, recall)	**Yes**	3.3.3
OL2000.1.7	Use address book to address mail	**Yes**	3.2.1
OL2000.1.8	Flag mail messages	No	3.2.4
OL2000.1.9	Navigate within mail	**Yes**	3.3.1
OL2000.1.10	Find messages	**Yes**	3.4.3
OL2000.1.11	Configure basic mail print options	**Yes**	3.3.2
OL2000.1.12	Work with attachments	**Yes**	3.2.3
OL2000.1.13	Add a signature to mail	**Yes**	3.4.2
OL2000.1.14	Customize the look of mail	No	3.4.1
OL2000.1.15	Use mail templates to compose mail	**Yes**	3.4.1
OL2000.1.16	Integrate and use mail with other Outlook components	No	3.5.2
OL2000.1.17	Customize menu and task bars	No	2.4.1, 2.4.2
OL2000.2	**Use Outlook 2000 to manage messages**		
OL2000.2.1	Create folders	**Yes**	2.3.3
OL2000.2.2	Sort mail	**Yes**	3.4.3
OL2000.2.3	Set viewing options	**Yes**	3.3.1
OL2000.2.4	Archive mail messages	**Yes**	3.4.4
OL2000.2.5	Filter a view	No	3.4.4
OL2000.3	**Use the Outlook 2000 calendar**		
OL2000.3.1	Navigate within the calendar	**Yes**	2.1.1
OL2000.3.2	Schedule appointments and events	**Yes**	2.1.2
OL2000.3.3	Set reminders	**Yes**	2.1.2
OL2000.3.4	Print in calendar	**Yes**	2.1.4
OL2000.3.5	Schedule multi-day events	**Yes**	2.1.2
OL2000.3.6	Configure calendar print options	No	2.1.4
OL2000.3.7	Customize the calendar view	No	2.1.1
OL2000.3.8	Schedule recurring appointments	**Yes**	2.1.2
OL2000.3.9	Customize menu and task bars	No	2.4.1, 2.4.2
OL2000.3.10	Add and remove meeting attendees	No	2.1.3
OL2000.3.11	Plan meetings involving others	**Yes**	2.1.3
OL2000.3.12	Save a personal or team calendar as a Web page	**Yes**	2.1.4
OL2000.3.13	Book office resources directly (e.g., conference rooms)	No	2.1.3
OL2000.3.14	Integrate calendar with other Outlook components	No	2.1.2

MOUS Standardized Performance	Activity	Performance Based	Advantage Series Chapter/Module
OL2000.4	**Navigate and use Outlook 2000 effectively**		
OL2000.4.1	Use Outlook Help and Office Assistant	**Yes**	1.4.1, 1.4.2
OL2000.4.2	Move items between folders	**Yes**	2.3.3
OL2000.4.3	Navigate between Outlook components	**Yes**	1.1.2
OL2000.4.4	Modify the Outlook Master Categories List	**Yes**	2.3.2
OL2000.4.5	Assign items to a category	**Yes**	2.3.1
OL2000.4.6	Sort information using categories	**Yes**	2.3.1
OL2000.4.7	Use the Office Clipboard	**Yes**	2.3.4
OL2000.5	**Use Contacts**		
OL2000.5.1	Create, edit, and delete contacts	**Yes**	1.2.1
OL2000.5.2	Send contact information via e-mail	**Yes**	3.5.2
OL2000.5.3	Organize contacts by category	**Yes**	2.3.1
OL2000.5.4	Manually record an activity in a journal	No	1.2.1
OL2000.5.5	Link activities to a contact	No	1.2.1
OL2000.5.6	Sort contacts using fields	No	1.2.2
OL2000.6	**Use Tasks**		
OL2000.6.1	Create and update one-time tasks	No	2.2.1
OL2000.6.2	Accept and decline tasks	**Yes**	2.2.3
OL2000.6.3	Organize tasks using categories	**Yes**	2.3.1
OL2000.6.4	Assign tasks to others	**Yes**	2.2.3
OL2000.6.5	Create tasks from other Outlook components	No	2.2.1
OL2000.6.6	Change the view for tasks	No	2.2.2
OL2000.7	**Integrate Office applications and other applications with Outlook 2000 components**		
OL2000.7.1	Create and use Office documents inside Outlook 2000	**Yes**	3.5.1
OL2000.8	**Use Notes**		
OL2000.8.1	Create and edit notes	**Yes**	1.3.1
OL2000.8.2	Organize and view notes	**Yes**	1.3.1
OL2000.8.3	Customize notes	No	1.3.2